PORTRAIT OF A

Miracle

Portrait of a *Miracle*

Life with and without sickle cell disease.

By Perry Collins

XULON PRESS

Xulon Press
2301 Lucien Way #415
Maitland, FL 32751
407.339.4217
www.xulonpress.com

© 2020 by Perry Collins

All rights reserved solely by the author. The author guarantees all contents are original and do not infringe upon the legal rights of any other person or work. No part of this book may be reproduced in any form without the permission of the author. The views expressed in this book are not necessarily those of the publisher.

Unless otherwise indicated, Scripture quotations taken from the Holy Bible, New International Version (NIV). Copyright © 1973, 1978, 1984, 2011 by Biblica, Inc.™. Used by permission. All rights reserved.

Printed in the United States of America.

Paperback ISBN-13: 978-1-6322-1616-8
eBook ISBN-13: 978-1-6322-1617-5

Portrait of a Miracle

Life with and without sickle cell disease.

By Perry Collins

XULON PRESS

Xulon Press
2301 Lucien Way #415
Maitland, FL 32751
407.339.4217
www.xulonpress.com

© 2020 by Perry Collins

All rights reserved solely by the author. The author guarantees all contents are original and do not infringe upon the legal rights of any other person or work. No part of this book may be reproduced in any form without the permission of the author. The views expressed in this book are not necessarily those of the publisher.

Unless otherwise indicated, Scripture quotations taken from the Holy Bible, New International Version (NIV). Copyright © 1973, 1978, 1984, 2011 by Biblica, Inc.™. Used by permission. All rights reserved.

Printed in the United States of America.

Paperback ISBN-13: 978-1-6322-1616-8
eBook ISBN-13: 978-1-6322-1617-5

This is a personal account of my life and the interaction of God in it. It is a life with and without sickle cell disease.

Dedication

To my lovely wife Shari, and my five beautiful daughters, Tina, Brittany, Brooke, Brandi, and Briana, whose presence in my life, whether fleeting or permanent, are a true sign of God's continued blessings on me and who inspire me every day.

Acknowledgments

My deepest love and gratitude to my wife Shari, who married me over thirty years ago despite my concerns about how my illness would affect her, including the very real risk that she would be left to mother our daughters without me.

Thanks to my daughters Tina, Brittany, Brooke, Brandi, and most recently Briana (whom we took in as our own eight years ago, after her mother passed)—you are all my special girls and I love each of you and pray every day for your continued success in life. I thank God daily for allowing me to live to see all of you grow into beautiful young women and prepare to launch yourselves into the world and experience your own exciting adventures. A special note to Tina, whose mother moved with her when she was twelve. I'm so happy that we have reconnected and I have the chance to witness the love and expansion of your own family. I think of you often and pray for your good health and happiness, and for the added blessing that we can now enjoy and share God's greatness together.

My thanks, too, to my old mother hen and big sister Emma Vernetta Ramsey, who watched over us kids, who taught me how to read, write, add, and subtract, and has been my spiritual cheerleader (and arguably the best cook I've ever known!), and to my sister Belinda, who invited me to live with her, and propelled my life in an entirely new, positive direction. I cannot fail to thank my best man, Rev. Larry Camper, who calls me constantly to see if I need help, to pray for me and encourage me almost daily to stay on the path God has set before me and to stay with this message and make it a finished work.

Finally, but foremost, my depthless gratitude for the blessings that God has bestowed on me. I endeavor to walk in His light and follow the path He has laid out for me.

With my thanks to these and all of my loved ones too numerous to list here, this is the most important lesson I have learned that I encourage you to keep in your heart and live by:

Stay with the Lord. Never let Him go, no matter where you find yourself.

INTRODUCTION

In this world today we find very little glimmers of hope among the many atrocities and calamities surfacing around us on a daily basis. It seems that destruction, hate, greed and jealousy are accelerating all around us at an alarming rate. One country seeks to deny the very existence of another. Parents are murdering their children. Children are murdering their parents. Citizens are murdered in the streets, in their cars and in their homes by one another as well as by the very ones who took an oath to protect and serve and there are no consequences for it. People will sell their souls for the almighty dollar. Through it all we walk around oblivious to the madness as if asleep. While seeking the word of God I found that He has already told us about it. 2 Timothy 3:1-5 states.

> "But mark this: There will be terrible times in the last days. People will be lovers of themselves, lovers of money, boastful, proud, abusive, disobedient to their parents, ungrateful, unholy, without love, unforgiving, slanderous, without self-control, brutal, not lovers of the good, treacherous, rash, conceited, lovers of pleasure rather than lovers of

God, having a form of godliness but denying its power. Have nothing to do with them.

Not only does He say that it's coming, but He tells us why it is coming, who is responsible for it and what we must do to protect ourselves. The "who" is found in Ephesians 6:12;

> "For we wrestle not against flesh and blood, but against principalities, against powers, against the rulers of the darkness of this world, against spiritual wickedness in high places."

The "why" is found in John 10:10;

> "The thief comes only to steal and kill and destroy. I came that they may have life, and have it abundantly."

"What we must do to protect ourselves" is in Ephesians 6:13-17;

> "[13] Therefore take up the whole armor of God, so that you may be able to withstand on that evil day, and having done everything, to stand firm. [14] Stand therefore, and fasten the belt of truth around your waist, and put on the breastplate of righteousness. [15] As shoes for your feet put on whatever will make you ready to proclaim the gospel of peace. [16] With all of these,[c] take the shield of faith, with which you will be able to quench all the flaming arrows

of the evil one. [17] Take the helmet of salvation, and the sword of the Spirit, which is the word of God."

Through it all He tells us that "He will never leave us or forsake us." Hebrews 13:5. Yet we still sleep. The enemy is busy escalating the madness at a feverish pace. Satan is desperate and he seeks to crush us in any and every way that he can. His goal is to make sure that when Jesus cracks the sky to collect His faithful that He doesn't have a single survivor standing on the battlefield. The thief comes but to kill steal and destroy. First he wants to kill your compassion and charitableness for others. How? By destroying your finances and keeping you pinned down fighting and scratching to keep your own head above the water. Then he wants to steal your joy. How? By hitting you with bad news around every corner and stirring you into a sea of hopelessness. And last he wants to destroy your very flesh. How? By coming at you with every manner of disease and infirmity that he can muster. Cancer, AIDS, Diabetes, Hypertension, Arthritis, Sickle Cell Disease, anything you can name all designed to take you out before you can complete the work that God has called you to. What has God called you to? There are primarily two things:

1. The great commandment–Matt. 22:37-40;

> "Jesus replied: 'Love the Lord your God with all your heart and with all your soul and with all your mind. This is the first and greatest commandment. And the second is like it: Love your neighbor as

yourself. All the Law and the Prophets hang on these two commandments.'"

2. The great commission–Mark 16:15-18;

"He said to them, 'Go into all the world and preach the good news to all creation. Whoever believes and is baptized will be saved, but whoever does not believe will be condemned. And these signs will accompany those who believe; In my name they will drive out demons; they will speak in new tongues; they will pick up snakes with their hands; and when they drink deadly poison, it will not hurt them at all; they will place their hands on sick people, and they will get well."

These are the things that He has called us to. And with faith the size of a mustard seed, we can accomplish it. You see that little word "faith" is the key to our success. Faith is the answer to satan's desperation. "Faith is the essence of things hoped for and the evidence of things not seen." Faith is the key that opens doors that no man can open or close. It is your faith that drives out demons of immorality and fornication. It is your faith that frees you from the clutches of alcoholism and drug abuse. It is your faith that puts cancer to flight, or regulates that blood pressure or diabetes. It was faith that took sickle cell anemia out of my life and made it a non-factor for over twenty-eight years. No hospital visits and no medications. The only logical explanation comes from the word of the master. Jesus says "your faith has made you whole". The apostle Paul tells us in Romans 10:17. "Consequently, faith comes from hearing the message, and the message is heard through the word of Christ."

This is the story of my life. The first half of which was riddled with terrifying and excruciatingly painful episodes accompanied by swelling, high fevers, chest congestion and pneumonia. The latter half was the evidence of a journey that can be nothing short of a miracle and a message of hope because God is the same yesterday, today and forever. It was a miracle that ultimately opened my eyes to the fact that God was watching over me and protecting me throughout my entire life and that, in fact, my life is a Portrait of Miracles.

apostle Paul tells us in Romans 10:17. "Consequently, faith comes from hearing the message, and the message is heard through the word of Christ."

This is the story of my life. The first half of which was riddled with terrifying and excruciatingly painful episodes accompanied by swelling, high fevers, chest congestion and pneumonia. The latter half was the evidence of a journey that can be nothing short of a miracle and a message of hope because God is the same yesterday, today and forever. It was a miracle that ultimately opened my eyes to the fact that God was watching over me and protecting me throughout my entire life and that, in fact, my life is a Portrait of Miracles.

Chapter One

I remember sitting at the window as a small child, watching my brothers and cousins play in the snow. I must have been about five years old and already it was apparent that I couldn't do the things that the rest of the kids could do. The wind and cold were generally unbearable for me to endure more than a few minutes at a time, no matter how much I bundled up. It only took a small exposure or slight overexertion of energy to bring on an episode that frightened me just to think about.

The pain was something that I couldn't describe or explain to anyone. It was pain that could not and would not be eased. Not even by the most loving and caring mother in the world. To be touched or caressed was often agonizing instead of soothing. Sometimes the mere sound of someone's voice would pierce me like a knife. So, rather than risk bringing on such an episode, I would sit by the window and gaze at the fun and frolic that everyone else was having.

One day, my brothers were building the biggest snow bear I had ever seen. It was so big that they needed to use a ladder to finish the head. They were having a ball, and I found myself laughing just as hard as they were.

Eventually, I would frequently be joined by my baby brother, David, the only other person in the world who could fully understand my plight, who also appeared to experience these mysterious pains and was slowly learning his limitations.

In spite of those frightening times, I have many wonderfully pleasant memories. I couldn't have been more than three or four years old when I was sitting in the dirt at the house my parents often referred to as the old Pusey place, after the name of the owners. It was a rather large, white house that was situated well back from the road, up a very long lane. I sat, playing under this huge brick chimney, with a small toy tractor. The warm sun and gentle breeze felt so good. I guess that's why I still remember it.

We had huge fields all around us, and every summer the migrant workers would come to pick the crops. Sometimes they would park along the edge of our property and they would have candy and sodas that they would sell to us. My mom still has a picture of my two younger brothers and me, sitting in the dirt, naked, in what looks to be a mud puddle. As we grew through our teens, that picture would periodically reappear. It got rather embarrassing at times.

Then there were the times when my older brothers and sisters were in school. I, along with my younger brothers, David and Darryl, were too young to go, so we spent the days with Grants. Grants was my maternal grandmother. She was a tall, slim lady, with smooth chestnut skin and American Indian features. We learned as we got older that she had quite a bit of Indian blood in her. It also dawned on me later that she only seemed so tall back then because we were so small. But she was a tough little lady, who not only raised fourteen kids of her own but also a good many of

Chapter One

her grandchildren. She had a way of always popping up on us just as we were getting into things that we shouldn't. We thought she was magical and could read our minds, but her spankings were very real. Still, we loved hanging out there together, and there was always something we could get excited about. It seemed like someone would always be dropping off these huge snapping turtles and we would tease them with a stick. They would snap at the stick so hard, sometimes they would cut it in half.

"You know if he gets a hold of your finger, he won't let go until the sun goes down," the adults invariably warned us.

Then there was cousin Sonny, who would frequently stop by with a rooster and put it in a fight with the one in Grants' yard. She had a big white rooster and it was mean. We had to keep an eye out for it when running around, playing, or it might decide to jump us. He would put them in a fight and they would go at it until one of them was knocked out. Usually it was the one he'd brought as a challenger. He would throw water on it to revive it and then load it back into its crate and take it home. I can recall only one time that his challenger actually won.

Then there was the occasional stray dog that would show up in the yard, and Princess, the beautiful red boxer, just was not having it. She was in a wired pen that seemed totally secure, but whenever another dog showed up, somehow she would always manage to get out. One day she came tearing around the house, and the other dog took off running. I was in her way and she just plowed right over me, like I was a leaf in the wind. I always admired her, and she may be one reason I'm so crazy about large dogs to this day.

The nearest neighbor was the Chess family and they were white. Little Steve was right around my age, so he would come up

3

to the door and yell, "Can Perry come out to play?" We would go off running into the fields, or up to the old barn, where he had great toys, like a tractor big enough for both of us to ride on, and you had to pedal it around. Then he had little toys we pushed around, and climbing this huge sand pile, we made little roads all over it.

Those were fun days. Our world seemed so enormous to us, as kids. With so many aunts, uncles, and cousins, we were always on the move. We loved regularly visiting Mom's brothers and sisters, except Robert, who was an army captain who piloted helicopters in Vietnam, and lived in New York with his wife and their daughter, Michaylla. We only got to see them occasionally, when he was on leave. Michaylla loved to come and visit her swarm of cousins on the Shore and she gave attention to each and every one of them, young or old. She was like a kid in a candy store. We, on the other hand, saw our cousins every day. Our neighborhood was filled with my dad's relatives and there were so many cousins, you just couldn't keep count. We loved each other like an extended family of brothers and sisters. We worked together, played together, and got into trouble together constantly.

It was around this time that I remember my mom and dad having a very serious conversation in the living room. Mom was crying and dad was trying to console her and I began to understand that her brother Robert was killed in Vietnam. He could have come out and retired but instead he opted to take on a third tour of duty. His helicopter had been shot down over enemy territory and he didn't survive. Mom and Dad called all of us in and we had prayer for Uncle Robert. I don't remember going to the funeral and I think I was too young at the time but I do remember taking note of his grave at my mom's old home church. I often heard talk of how much of a great guy he was.

Sometimes we would spend days at Aunt Judy's house. Mom had started working at Green Giant, and mornings when she dropped the three of us off, David and I would calmly head for the house. I was happy to hang out and play with my cousin Lance all day and we started school at the same time. It was always nice to see his friendly face. Darryl, on the other hand, would cry and scream at her for leaving him there. She would generally try to give us something to appease us, so she could go peacefully, usually an apple, orange, pear, or an occasional piece of candy.

One morning, after being handed an apple, Darryl went into his routine with a vengeance. He fell to the ground, kicking and shrieking. Mom ignored him and began to back the car out of the yard, which only increased his screams, and curse words filled the air. When she reached the road, he leaped to his feet and ran after her, hurling his apple as hard as he could toward the car. It bounced and hit the target. That was the final straw. Mom shifted gears and pulled back up the driveway, at which point Darryl realized that maybe he had gone one step too far this time. When she jumped out of the car, he bolted for the house, but he only made it as far as the door when she grabbed hold of him. After that, I don't remember him throwing quite as many fits when she left us to go to work.

Chapter Two

I can't remember when I first began to show signs of being sick, but according to my mom, it was very early on. Even before I was old enough to tell her how I felt, she talked of my having high fevers and screaming relentlessly for days. Often, my legs hurt so badly that not only could I not walk but I couldn't even bear for my feet to touch the floor, and Mom would have to carry me from place to place on her back. On those occasions when David and I would get sick around the same time, she really had her hands full, because even though she might be up the entire night tending to us, she still had to go to work.

My mother's love and devotion to us, and to God, certainly was the sustaining force that kept my brother and I from becoming just another statistic. In those days, one out of two children with this affliction didn't live to become a teenager. She would often pray while rubbing me down with alcohol or sitting with David in her arms, trying to rock him to sleep. Sometimes my brother Mike, sensing Mom was tired, would pitch in and volunteer to rub the alcohol on us. He always seemed to be the one most concerned when we were in pain and usually stuck very close to us and mom. It's apparent to me now that God was always there, listening to her pray. Even with David and I sick so often, she didn't neglect our brothers and sisters. I don't know how she managed, but she always kept us fed and clothed. When we got hungry in between meals, we could usually find something in the cabinets or refrigerator.

She would clean houses and work in the fields for the white people who had large farms and houses. Sometimes she would take us with her and we would sit and play in the dirt or go off and explore while she and some of her sisters labored. These ladies could do everything that a man could do, and more.

We would ride on the back of the big farm trucks while they drove from field to field or to the store for lunch. Usually Mom and Aunt Judy drove; they could handle anything on wheels, and when we were old enough, they taught us how to drive the trucks and tractors. Their hard work paid off in a number of ways. The farmers and their wives always remembered us on special holidays, and would bring gifts or extra food to the house. Later, when we got old enough, they hired us.

Mom and her sisters were sweet, but at the same time they were tough on us, and made sure we behaved ourselves and understood that some things could harm us, and that all actions generally had consequences. Still, as energetic, growing, and curious kids, we had to learn many lessons for ourselves. I'm reminded of the time I had a run-in with a live-wire fence. The farmers quite often ran electric wires along the top of their fences to keep the livestock in check.

One day, my older brother Kenny and I were playing at one end of the field while Mom and her sisters were in the field's rows, picking the crops. Kenny gingerly touched the wire with a stick and nothing happened. So, I assumed that as long as there was something, a buffer, between my hand and the wire I would be safe. I picked up a leaf as large as my hand and grabbed the wire. It lit me up like a Christmas tree! Worse, I wasn't able to let go. Kenny jumped back and began yelling for Mom. That's when I really panicked and managed to yank my hand free of the wire. I ran to Kenny and tried to cover his mouth with my good hand, pleading with him not to tell Mom what had happened. He paused and swiftly looked me over for any sign of damage. Reassured that I was in fact OK, he relaxed. We never did tell Mom what had happened. I'd learned my lesson well and never toyed with a hot wire again.

Mom was and is the rock that has kept us together as a family. I never understood until I became an adult why Mom would so often force David and I out to church and Sunday school while the rest of the boys weren't pushed as hard to go. She feared for our lives and prayed and looked to God constantly for our refuge.

One Sunday, after Mom forced me to go to the service, I came home upset and told her I didn't want to go to church anymore because the preacher stood up in front of everyone and hollered at me. She laughed and explained that the preacher wasn't annoyed at me, that he was just excited about God's "good news." So, one day, not long after that, I sat down with the Bible and decided to read for myself some of God's good news. The Bible was so thick that I couldn't envision reading the whole thing, so I skipped to the end, thinking that must surely be where the most good news would be found. I managed to get more than halfway through the Book of Revelations before I had to put it down, scared to death. My spirit was trying to absorb what I was reading, even though I was terrified. It changed my life in many ways from that moment, because I immediately made up my mind that hell was one place I didn't ever want to end up.

We lived across the road from the church and we often played in the churchyard, treating it like an extension of our property. The church doors were never locked and we often went inside to admire it and drink in the eerie feeling of power and reverence that pervaded it, always careful not to touch or disturb anything. God, we felt, was always present there in the sanctuary and so we were always very quiet when we entered.

One day, mom asked me to walk over to the church with her, an unusual request because it was in the middle of a weekday. A lady I didn't recognize greeted us. Mom introduced us and then began to tell her how sick I sometimes got. The lady held my shoulders and began to pray aloud, which struck me as very strange, because we were the only ones in the church.

When we headed back home, mom explained that the lady was some kind of prophet and that her prayers were very powerful. I never saw her again, or heard anything about her, and I have no idea where she came from. But Mom always taught us that God was our help and our strength, and that He always heard our prayers. She planted the seeds that later sprang forth and took root, forming the foundation of my faith today.

My dad worked at an old sawmill and it seemed he was gone most of the time. He also worked on cars with my Uncle Oliver in his spare time, usually on weekends. He didn't have a huge role in raising us around the house, but he was the major provider for the family, and if things got too tight, he would dig down deep to find a way to keep us going. His hard work provided him a good support system to call upon when we were in trouble. His boss, at the sawmill, had a large hand in helping my dad build us a new house to live in. Although a bit more thin and frail now, back then Dad was a short but rather stout man and solid as a rock. Once in a while he would come home in a cheerful and somewhat inebriated mood, stand in the middle of the floor and, holding his arms out, challenge all of us to try and pull his arms down. No matter how many of us piled onto him, I don't recall his arms ever coming down. He never punished us very often directly, as it would terrify us just to hear Mom say, "Just wait until your daddy comes home." Just his yelling at us it was worse than Mom's spankings. At the same time, as long as he felt we were in the right, he always had our backs.

Chapter Three

In our new home we finally got indoor plumbing and running water. The boys' room had four bunk beds for the seven of us, instead of the two little twin beds we'd shared in the old house. Belinda and Vernetta had the girls' room to themselves as usual because I was too young remember when my older sister Margaret still lived with us. Although the times when she would come home for a visit with her husband, I was always reminded by Mom and my sisters that I was Margaret's favorite brother. They would tell me how she would spoil me as a baby, and even when I was no longer the baby of the house, she once took my punishment for me because she wrapped herself around me protectively and refused to let Mom get to me. I don't know what I had done, but Mom still tells everyone I was the worst, stubbornest child she had, that she had a terrible time getting me to keep my clothes on, with me often pulling them off as fast as she could put them on.

When Mom just had to be away, she would have my sister's help tend to us. My sister Vernetta was the youngest of my three sisters, but seemed to do the most to help keep tabs on her seven younger brothers. My sisters were so quick and rugged that even our bigger boy cousins didn't want to tangle with them too often when we were all outside playing. Belinda was sweet and bubbly most of the time, but she had a temper that could flare up in an instant. She wasn't very pretty when she was angry. Vernetta, on the other hand, was steadier and more predictable. She was like an old mother hen always keeping watch over us. You didn't usually have trouble with her unless you approached her directly or messed with her brothers. She had taught me how to read and write by the time I started kindergarten and I excelled through school despite missing so many days due to illness. School was usually fun for me. My cousin Mona and I are the same age and we spent many days together at the Grants' house before we were old enough for school. Mona was extremely bright as a child and excelled beyond me, which was surprising because she disliked school. I don't ever remember her getting anything but straight A's and she probably missed as many days as I did, though she wasn't always ill. She refused to let anyone separate us the entire time we were in elementary school. The first time they attempted to put us in separate classrooms was the second grade. Mona cried the entire day, refusing to do anything until and unless we were reunited. From that point, until we reached the sixth grade, the teachers kept us together.

My cousins Mona, Patricia, Alex, and I were really tight friends, even though we didn't all come together until we started kindergarten. Alex's and my birthdays were exactly one week apart, and so we always got together to celebrate. McDonald's was brand new in Salisbury then and my mom would take us there for burgers, fries, and milkshakes. It was an experience he and I have never forgotten. Alex was a super athlete and in my eyes he could do

anything. I use to marvel as he walked tirelessly around the yard on his hands. He was the first one of us I ever saw do a no-hands flip.

As a ball player, Alex was exceptional. Baseball and basketball were the number one and two pastimes in our neighborhood, with football a close third. During the summer we would spend our entire day at the ballpark, unless it rained or we had to work in the fields. Sometimes we would play baseball, basketball, and football all in the same day, and if that didn't wear us out, we would break out into free-for-all wrestling or run into a nearby field and have dirt-throwing wars. Sometimes we'd get so filthy, we were afraid to go home. We would have to race home in hopes of getting cleaned up before Mom or Dad arrived. Still, these were times when, sooner or later, those pains would arrive and I would be forced to retreat, to go home and lie down to weather the storm. Despite these episodes, my mom never tried to over-shelter me or discourage me from trying anything I wanted to do.

Chapter Four

Growing up in Oaksville was perhaps the most pleasurable experience of my life. We were all related in some way or another, and I had so many cousins to hang out with, you couldn't count them. Along with the Collins family, there were the Fishers, the Stewarts, the Halls, the Corbins, the Crumps, the Canons, the Fields, the Haywards, the Kings, the Miles, and even though they didn't live right in our neighborhood, the Cottman kids spent lots of time with us. Lionel and Nelson spent so much time with us it was as if they had become two more brothers to us. Most of our families were very large, and my family standing then at seven boys and three girls was right around the top.

We would always make our plans for the afternoon while working in the fields that morning, and one morning we sent out word that we would play baseball that afternoon. When we got home, we would typically hurry and change into our athletic wear and maybe grab a little refreshment or something. Then someone would yell, "Last one to the park is a rotten egg!" and we'd tear out of the house and race for the park. Darryl and I, that day, were in the lead and pretty much neck in neck. I had no intention of letting him win because I knew he'd never let me live it down. But suddenly as we reached the driveway to the ballpark, we bounced off something and slammed to the ground. Someone had strung a barely visible barbed wire across the driveway and it had caught us right across the top of our chests. A couple of the barbs had torn my skin and there was a little blood, but we were ok. Had the wire been just a little higher, or we a little shorter, it could have caught us around the neck, which, at the speed with which we had flung ourselves into it, could have been fatal.

When the news reached the adults, the entire neighborhood was thrown into an uproar. My dad was furious, and when he found out the culprit was Mr. Walter, who lived across the street from the park and generally disliked kids, he wanted to hurt him badly. My mom begged and pleaded for him not to go after him, but other men in the community got to Mr. Walter first. They yelled and screamed at him, threatening that if anything like that ever happened again, they would have him arrested. They made sure he knew that he had no authority over the park and that it belonged to the neighborhood, that the kids were to have full access at all times. Although he didn't like kids, his wife, Ms. Frances, was head over heels in love with all of us. She sold candy, soda, and ice cream out of her house and we kept her in business throughout our childhood. On the rare occasion she wasn't there when we came by, Mr. Walter would come out to serve us. He made no attempt to hide the fact that he wasn't happy about it, but he would never turn down the chance to take our money. I still have the marks on my chest to this day from the barbed wire, but I think of it as just one more reminder of the great community I grew up in.

Like many neighborhoods and family environments, there were the inevitable rivalries and feuds. Sometimes the fights were downright scary. I thank God that, in those days, if we had to get physical to settle things, we invariably used our hands instead of reaching for more life-threatening weapons. There were maybe one or two occasions where somebody went too far and grabbed their daddy's shotgun to install fear into an altercation, but even then I don't think there was ever any real intent to harm on the agenda. Most of the time we stuck together, and most of the other neighborhoods and town folk knew not to mess with any of us unless they were willing to deal with all of us. Frequently, we would hear "There go them Oaksville boys again." We weren't the type of kids who went out looking for trouble, but we weren't the type to turn tail and run either.

We had a local baseball team called the Oaksville Eagles, which became very popular around Maryland's Eastern Shore. Sundays in the summer time were bustling with church services, camp meetings, and afternoon baseball games. Hotdogs for a quarter, sodas for a dime, ice cream cones, and penny candy all helped to make the days enjoyable.

One of the more infamous days was one particular Sunday, when my brother Darryl, a year younger than me, was almost killed. It started out as an average Sunday where, after church, everyone gathered at the ballfield for the regular afternoon game and other fun. As kids, we ran, wrestled, played tag, chased down foul balls, and did anything else we could think of to have fun.

Now, the local team had a large, very old bat that they used for swinging practice while waiting in the on-deck circle, where the next player stood while awaiting his turn at bat. The old bat had a steel spike driven into the center of it to give it added weight. Swinging the old weighted bat first meant that when you stepped into the batter's box with your favorite bat, it felt as light as a feather. This was real baseball and some of the pitchers these guys had to face were the real deal. So, this practice was designed to give an added edge to the batter so that he could get his swing around in a hurry.

Unfortunately, while our cousin Beverly was taking his practice swings, the spike dislodged from the bat and flew over the backstop fence. We were standing around talking, joking, and horse playing, when someone suddenly shrieked, "Look Out!"

As we looked around curiously, Darryl abruptly collapsed, his hands reaching behind his head. Blood seeped through his fingers. It was clear that he needed medical attention quick.

Beverly came tearing around the dugout and when it became clear how bad the gash in his head was, he picked Darryl up and jumped into his car to take him home. We all followed, tearing down the road on foot. The ball park was only about a quarter mile from our house and we were used to running it all the time. Minutes after we got home, an ambulance arrived. They swiftly strapped Darryl to the stretcher and loaded him inside, peeling away, the siren screaming. Beverly insisted on riding with Darryl in the ambulance, so Mom and Dad jumped into the car and headed out behind them. A large group of us stood in the yard silently watching as the vehicles disappeared.

As the sound of the siren dissipated, we heard another distress signal. We turned to see my younger brother David clutching his chest and moaning. He was having one of his dreaded episodes. All we could do was try and calm him down by telling him that everything was going to be all right and that Darryl would be coming back soon. We took him into the house and had him lie down to try to relax, while we all sat quietly, waiting on the news about Darryl.

It was rather late in the evening when Mom and Dad returned home. With them was Darryl, with a big bald spot cut into the back of his afro and a large bandage inside it. The doctors told my parents that if the spike had landed less than an inch further to the right, it would have killed him. We had been blessed yet again, and in more ways than one it turned out. By insisting David lie down and be quiet, his pains were short-lived, lasting only for an hour or two. And our cousin Beverly took care of the hospital bill, returning several times to check on Darryl and bring him a gift.

Although the doctors had warned Mom that neither David nor I would probably live to see our teenage years, it was Darryl who appeared to be most at risk and unlikely to survive his childhood. He was always falling out of trees onto his back while swinging from branch to branch. One time he crashed head-on into our older brother in the dark, who was on his bike. The handlebars met Darryl's two front teeth with a sickening crash and knocked them out. We kids thought he was young enough to grow a new set, but he never did. And I'm pretty sure it was Darryl who ran out into the street one day, chasing the ball we were playing with, just as a huge Showel chicken-feed truck was barreling around the bend. The driver saw him dart into the road and slammed on the brakes. Our cousin, Elmer was working in the field directly in front of our house and immediately reacted, somehow managing to leap off the tractor, race toward Darryl ahead of the truck, and snatch him up in one arm while using his other arm as a buffer between them and the truck's grill. That truck pushed them a good five or ten feet before it managed to stop, but Cousin Elmer was big enough to withstand the truck's push whereas Darryl would probably have been crushed. Needless to say, we were always a bit afraid for the boy. Still, life was good in the old neighborhood.

The ballpark was not the only place we played through the years. We played in each other's yards, out in the fields next to our homes, and sometimes right down the middle of the road, although that meant we had to be on the lookout for speeding cars.

One day we decided to play football in our yard—it was the last time I ever had a real interest in playing that particular sport; I did play again, but never with quite the same enthusiasm. I was running with the ball and I got tackled. I went down on my left knee.

Pop!

I got to my feet, despite the sharp pain, and tried to hop to the house on one leg. A couple of my brothers caught up with me to see where I was hurt. Looking down, I saw my kneecap twisted way over toward the inside of my leg. I freaked out and my brothers scooped me up and carried me into the house. Mom took one look at my leg and grabbed her purse, telling my brothers to put me in the car.

When we got to the hospital, I was so scared. I didn't know what to do. The doctors looked at my leg and sent me off to have it x-rayed. The x-rays showed a line across the kneecap

"It's fractured," the doctor said. "We'll need to put it in a cast." The nurse came in to get me ready and moved my injured leg to one side. I screamed and my bladder just let go. I peed not only on myself but her as well. She wasn't upset, and helped me clean myself up.

Once the cast was on, it wasn't so bad. It was fun being the center of attention at school. Everyone came up asking to sign it, and there was no shortage of kids lending a helping hand to get me around more comfortably. The bus ride was a little awkward, because I needed a seat on the right-side aisle of the bus so my leg could fully extend, since I couldn't bend it. It felt like a long six weeks, but when they removed the cast, my kneecap had shifted back to where it belonged, the only evidence of its displacement being the cast, which of course still bulged on the inside where it had shifted to after the accident. I kept that cast as a souvenir for many years.

Chapter Five

Our schools became integrated by the time I was in the fourth grade and we got along pretty well with our white classmates, although it wasn't quite as smooth for my older brothers, as there were more confrontations with the older boys. They had sit-ins, and lunch boycotts, and if anyone, black or white, got caught traveling to the bathroom alone, they usually came back bloody or bruised.

Most of my time in elementary school, however, I enjoyed being the teacher's pet. I was often sick and so tiny, but no one dared to pick on me because someone bigger would always stand up for me.

When I entered junior high school though, I managed to get into some real trouble and found myself in the principal's office. I was found guilty of something that Principal Williams detested most, which he called "third-partying." I had told one of the girls in my class something that I'd heard another girl say about her, and before the day was gone, the two girls got into a real knock-down, drag-out fight. Mr. Williams was so mad at me that he gave me a choice: corporal punishment with "The Boss" or three days' suspension. I knew that if I went home and had to face my parents, having been suspended from school, it would be the most miserable three days of my entire life, so I chose to face The Boss instead. The Boss was a wooden paddle over two inches thick, with a round handle. It had holes drilled into it so that when it landed on your hand or your backside, it sucked your flesh into it like a vacuum. He also gave me the choice of where I wanted it. I chose the backside. Moments later, I found myself wishing I had taken the suspension, because I could hardly sit down for the next three days. I certainly learned my lesson though, about not being a third-party instigator.

When I was thirteen, my oldest sister, Margaret, who lived in New Jersey with her husband and two kids and was pregnant with number three, got sick and developed pneumonia. When they sent her home from the hospital, she suffered a miscarriage and hemorrhaged to death. I had just recently written her a letter reminding her that my birthday was coming, but she had never written me back. I didn't learn until then that our birthdays were so close. My birthday is March 6 and her birthday was March 17. That could have been why I was her favorite. When Mom and Dad went to the funeral in New Jersey, my sister Vernetta went with them while the rest of us remained at home. When they came home, they brought me a letter that Margaret had written in response to mine but had never had the chance to mail. I can't remember now what ever happened to the letter, but I had always intended to keep it. Even so, I will never forget my sister, who left us just too soon.

Margaret's passing brought a change to our lives, the arrival of her two children to live with us. My niece, Gay, was about eight years old and my nephew, Tyrone, was about four. From that point onward, they became another brother and sister to us. Gay was mischievous and mean, and as a result she was constantly in trouble, from the moment she arrived. Less than half an hour after her arrival, she hit my brother Michael in the back with a metal pipe. She seemed to have a very strange concept of what was right and what was wrong.

It was summer when they came to live with us and their first trip to the ballpark was as eventful as the first day they came to live with us. Our cousin Aretha was Gay's age and she approached Gay very timidly, with her hands clutched to her chest, trying to greet her. Aretha burst into tears. We asked Gay what happened, she replied, "She came up to me with her hands up, and I thought she wanted to fight." Needless to say, we had to keep a very close watch on her whenever we went out playing or visiting.

Tyrone was very young when his mom passed, and as time went on, he didn't appear to remember much about her. He would cling to Dad, no matter where Dad was or what he was doing. He would spend an hour every night sitting on Dad's shoulders while Dad read the paper. We thought it was cute, but none of us would ever dare to try it.

Gay, on the other hand, remembered her mom very well and one night we found out just how much she missed her. We were all sitting in the living room this particular night, watching television, and Gay was sitting on the floor, playing with her doll. Without warning, the front door opened. There was no wind—it was as if someone just opened it. Gay looked up and said, "Mommy, how nice of you to come by and see us." We exchanged looks and every one of us except Gay stood and left the room, including my dad, to give Gay and her mom all the time together that they wanted. I don't know who eventually returned to shut the door, but it wasn't going to be me. That was the last time I was aware of something like this happening, but I still think of Margaret regularly, to this day.

As I got older, our family's growing pains became more and more evident. It seems I was always fighting with my younger brother Darryl, who wanted to prove that he was stronger or better than me. However, I wasn't the only one. My older brothers were perpetually having to put him in check. But they also were beginning to challenge the authority of Vernetta, our sister, who was in charge when mom and dad were not home. By the time I became a teenager, my brother Larry had decided that Vernetta was no longer permitted to tell him what to do. Typically, if we did something we weren't supposed to, Vernetta would scold us and sometimes spank us, and we would run off, crying. But this time, when she hit Larry, he turned and hit her back. This prompted a severe whipping, and before we knew it, they were in a full-fledged brawl that seemed to go on for hours. She would beat him and walk away. He would lie there for a moment, recovering, and then get up and tie into her again. After this played over and over again, Vernetta looked exhausted and we were pleading for them to stop. Still, Larry refused to quit and she refused to let him win, until Vernetta collapsed on the floor and our cousin Levi came in, scooped her up, and laid her on the couch. We fanned her and gave her water and after a few minutes she was ok again. That was the worst incident of sibling rivalry I can remember between any of the ten of us. It not only terrified me but it must have scared both Vernetta and Larry, because they never went at each other that way again, ever.

Overall, we were a very tightly knit family. Mom and Dad taught us to always look out for each other. They also taught us how to work and save for what we wanted in life. As small children, all the way up until we each left home, we worked in the fields, picking cucumbers, tomatoes, beans, strawberries, watermelons, and anything else the farmers would pay us for. We also loaded and drove the tractors and trucks to take the crops to market. We cleaned chicken houses, cut grass, and loaded and stacked baled hay.

One thing I had a huge problem with was snakes. They terrified me. We frequently ran across them while working the fields. It got to the point where we could tell if one was near by the smell in the air. It was a sweet smell, like that of fruit or freshly mowed grass. One day, early in the morning, we went out to pick beans, and shortly before noon I came across an empty fertilizer bag amid the rows I was working. The hair on the back of my neck stood up as I was greeted by that disturbingly familiar smell. My first instinct was to keep moving, keep picking, and ignore the bag, but I knew I had to make sure there was no danger. I grabbed a small stick, wedged it under the edge of the bag, and flipped the bag over to reveal the biggest, broadest snake I had ever seen. I leaped back and screamed "Snake!" over and over, as I dashed toward the safety of the road. Luckily, that morning was chilly and the snake was lethargic and in no mood to give chase. My brothers and cousins came running and found it just where I had discovered it and killed it. There was no way I was going back in the field that day, so I walked the six or seven miles home.

Sometimes we would worry about meeting up with dogs on the road, but my fear of slithering creatures far outweighed any fear of dogs. I've loved dogs all of my life; I have never been able to tolerate a snake anywhere near me.

We shared the money we earned with Mom to help pay for necessities. Most of the time we bought our own school clothes and supplies, and periodically we might splurge on some candy or toys. Some days we would walk from the various fields to our grandmother's house and wait there for Mom or Dad to pick us up. And sometimes we would walk home from Grants' house, if we were anxious to get to the ballpark.

One day, Eddie, Clark, Darryl, David, and I decided to walk home, but we were worried because one of the white neighbors in that community owned two large German Shepherds, which were rumored to be attack dogs, so, as a precaution, we scouted around for some large sticks and rocks for protection. Sure enough, less than a quarter mile from the owner's house, we spotted the dogs emerging from the woods opposite. They stayed on their side of the road, watching us all the while. We did the same, never taking our eyes off of them. Once they were comfortably behind us, they turned and charged at us, snarling and growling. We wheeled around and fired every weapon we had at them at the same time, causing them to stop in their tracks. They turned and bolted in the opposite direction. Relieved, we laughed and celebrated all the way home. After that, we always made sure we walked with some kind of defensive weapon in hand for protection. Despite that experience, the dogs had impressed me, and the German Shepherd became my favorite breed of all dogs. Their markings were beautiful and they were very smart animals.

We had a few mixed breeds that were great family dogs. Rosco, Bosco, Bandit, and Bullet were among our favorites and they were each a German Shepherd mix. Bullet was the biggest, fastest, and prettiest dog I had ever seen, jet black, with a shiny, wavy coat, and

Chapter Five

when I say he was fast, that's no exaggeration. Someone once let him run alongside their car and accelerated up to forty miles per hour before Bullet started to lose ground. He followed us everywhere, whether we wanted him to or not. He was gentle and smart, and so strong that one day we tied him to Dad's boat before going to school to keep him from following us. When we got home later that day, he had pulled the boat halfway across the yard.

Bullet was also very protective. One day our cousin Bud came into our yard. He and Dad were great friends, and he loved to play with us. He'd toss us into the air and catch us. That day he grabbed Tyrone, our nephew, and as he held him up in the air, Bullet gently but firmly grabbed Bud by the seat of his pants and would not let go until Cousin Bud put Tyrone down.

Sadly, after a few years, Bullet was hit by a car and seriously injured. We were so upset that Dad picked him up and he and Mom went off to find a vet. They returned a few hours later with Bullet wrapped in a black plastic bag. Dad explained that he had suffered internal injuries and that his leg was beyond repair, that even if the doctor had removed the leg, there was still no guarantee he would survive, so they had to have him put to sleep. We were brokenhearted. The next day we went out and buried him in our field, in an area that was never plowed.

Darryl, meanwhile, had been helping Aunt Bella with her dog Lady, a purebred German Shepherd. She'd had puppies and he was helping to take care of them until they were weaned. After the pups reached six weeks old, Aunt Bella let Darryl pick one to take home. It was our first purebred dog, and I don't know if it was the luck of the draw or if it was the seven boys drilling the dog day and night, but Major became the most fantastic dog we had ever seen. He came to know everything we said, he knew the name of everybody in the house, and there was no place we would go that he wouldn't go. By the time he was six months old, he was getting bigger and stronger every day. We would race him around the house, through the house, and all over our property. One day Darryl, David, and I were running between the kitchen to the bedroom, with Major on our heels. We would jump onto the top bunk, as that was the only place he couldn't reach us, and laugh as he stood and barked at us. After a couple of times, Major leaped up alongside us. From then on there was nowhere we could run that he couldn't follow. We would run over the tops of old junked cars, jump ditches, and climb hills and he would always be there. We could play Hide and Seek with him and all we had to say was, "Major, go find Darryl" or whoever was hiding and he would put his nose down and go right to where the person was hiding. We tried tricking him by having several of us hide at the same time, but whoever you told him to find, that was the one that he went to.

Major loved to play basketball with us and we would play Keep-away, passing the ball back and forth between us. We would run him so long and hard that, when it was over, he would find a water puddle to lie down in to cool off, lying down on his belly with his legs spread out, like a bullfrog. Unfortunately, it got to where he would sink his teeth into the ball and take off running with it. We finally had to tie him up before we could start a game with our cousins.

His protective instinct was phenomenal and it got to where we had to be very careful with what we told him to do. If we said, "Get him," and it wasn't one of our family, he would growl at them first, as a warning, and if they didn't leave right away, he would get very aggressive. If we got in trouble with Mom, all we had to do was run outside. If she chased us with a switch or belt, Major would run alongside her, jumping up and down, trying to take it away from her. Sometimes she would get mad and turn on him. Because she was family and he would never hurt one of us, he would turn tail and run for cover. After a while, Mom got wiser and decided she wasn't going to chase us anymore. She would say, "Sooner or later, you'll come in to eat or sleep. Either way, I won't forget that I owe you." She wasn't kidding. We soon learned that if we ran, we got more than we would have gotten had we stood and taken our medicine the first time. Major loved Mom as much as us boys though, and whenever she went out to hang clothes on the line, or to talk to someone who came into the yard, he would be right by her side. You could talk to her if you were a stranger, but Major wouldn't permit anyone to touch her. Not even a handshake.

Aunt Bella stopped by one day to show Mom her new car. As they were standing, talking, Major took his place beside her. Finally, Aunt Bella looked at him

"Elsie, this old crazy dog call his self being your bodyguard?"

Major immediately looked at her and gave a low grumble, a growl.

"Bella, be careful," Mom warned. "He knows everything you say."

"Yeah, ain't nobody scared of that old crazy mutt."

Major looked up at Mom, whining as if asking for her permission to intervene. Aunt Bella got into her new car and began backing out of the yard. When she reached the street, Mom look at Major.

"You can go get her now, if you want to," she said softly. Major took off and leaped onto the hood of Aunt Bella's new car, scratching furiously at the windshield, trying to reach her. Mom tried unsuccessfully to summon him back, but he wanted Aunt Bella to know that he didn't appreciate her talking about him.

"My car! My car!" Aunt Bella kept shouting. After that, she never had any harsh words for him while he was guarding Mom.

My brother Moon got a big kick out of intelligent interaction with Major. He always called him the "Humanoid." Sometimes, it seemed like Major got offended if you called him a dog.

One night we were sitting around the kitchen table and Jack popped in for a visit. He and Moon were in conversation about something and they got into a passionate disagreement. When Moon got too frustrated to deal with him, he looked at Major, who was sitting on the floor beside him, and said, "Just tell Jack to be quiet."

Major looked at Jack and gave him a half whine, half bark, as if to say, "You heard the man."

Jack immediately protested, saying, "Oh man, you want to play with that dog? I'm not playing with him. I'm done." He got up and went into the living room and sat down to watch TV.

"We're not finished yet," Moon called after him. "Ain't no need to get up and run. Get on back in here."

"No man, I ain't coming back in there. You want to play with that dog."

Moon looked at Major. "Go bring him back in here."

Major got up and went straight into the living room, stood in front of Jack and started whining, and wouldn't stop until Jack got up and walked back into the kitchen. He sat down and refused to say a word.

Major's aggression did get a little out of hand after a while, and eventually we discovered that a couple of Eddie's little brothers next door had been teasing him when we left him chained up outside. We woke up to Major having some sort of fit outside and spotted one or two of the kids by the back door of their house, jumping and taunting him. It made him crazy. Every time he would see one of them outside, he would chase them back into their house. We had to start admonishing him more and more whenever he became aggressive. It was difficult for him, because he understood normal conversation, and if that conversation involved him, he couldn't help but react.

Then something strange happened. Vernetta and, Eddie's older sister, Vera, were standing in the back doorway, talking. Major was watching them.

"Why is that stupid dog staring at us?" Vera demanded. Instead of charging at her, Major turned and went over to the clothes line, picked up the pole Mom would use to prop up the line, and came back to stand in front of them, shaking the pole from side to side, the pole repeatedly slamming into his flank with force, seemingly wanting to let her know that he wanted to beat her with a stick.

"Look at him!" she scoffed. "See? I told you he was crazy!"

By this time he was shaking the stick so hard, it was beating him on both sides, and he began to growl ominously. When she ignored him, he dropped the stick and charged at her at full speed. She and Vernetta leaped inside, barely shutting the door on him in time. From that point on he would look for something to shake before getting aggressive, and we swiftly learned to calm him down when he started shaking things in his mouth.

The straw that broke the camel's back was one day when I was out playing with him in the front yard. He would do backflips in the air whenever he caught a stick or his favorite ball. On one of his flips he came down and then froze, his gaze locked on the yard next door. Eddie's little brother Tre' was in the middle of their yard, staring back. Before I could react, Tre' tore off toward his front door. Major bolted after him, with me screaming, "Major! No!" Major paid no attention. He caught Tre' at his doorstep, jerked him to the ground, released him, and proudly trotted back to me as if to say, "Ha, you didn't get away that time."

Tre', meanwhile, leaped to his feet, and raced into his house, shrieking, "He bit me! He bit me!"

While Major had grabbed him to pull him to the ground, he had inadvertently broken the skin just slightly on his leg. If he'd intended to hurt Tre', he could have mauled him, on the spot. Instead, he just yanked him off his feet and trotted away. However, Tre' had to be taken to the doctor to be checked out. All of Major's health records were in order and Tre' was in no real danger. Still, the whole neighborhood was upset about it by then, because Major had a bad reputation. I felt badly, because I should have been able to stop him in his tracks, but my yell to him had been made more out of fear than as a firm command to cease immediately.

After that, we practiced commands to halt him in his tracks, and whenever he showed aggression, we stopped him immediately, and we began keeping him inside the house, with us, versus leaving him outside. After a while he only responded protectively when he was in the house, something we got a good glimpse of when my

Chapter Five

brother Larry, who had joined the Marines and had never gotten to really know Major, came home after a few years in a surprise visit. He came to the back door and met Major on the steps. Major challenged him, but sensed Larry was somehow part of the family and let Larry chase him away from the door and enter. That evening, he decided to hit the town and hang out with old friends, and didn't return until we were all in bed. Major was lying on my bed, at my feet, where he often slept. When Larry entered the house, Major started to whine and I woke up. When Larry stepped into the bedroom, Major froze him in his tracks. All we could see were these green eyes glowing in the dark, accompanied by the deepest, most threatening growl I had ever heard. I tried to calm him down, but he was adamant that Larry was not allowed in the boys' room.

Larry backed out of the room and slept on the couch, later often joking that he had chosen to sleep on the couch to keep from killing our animal. Still, I believe he understood how serious Major was about not allowing him to stay in the bedroom. After a day or two, they came to an understanding and Major was less guarded when Larry came and went, and even after Larry returned to base, the next time he came home they didn't have any problems with each other.

I adored Major and he was devoted to all of us. He would follow us as a group or he would follow if one of us wandered off alone. One day my brother Darryl and I had a fight and I was so angry at him that when Mom and Dad came home, I was still ranting and raving about it. Mom tried to calm me down, but I wasn't hearing it, so Dad stepped in and yelled, "Shut it down, now!" None of us ever dared challenge him, so I immediately shut my mouth. Still fuming, as soon as I could do so, I strode out of the house and down the road. It was dark but I didn't care, I was so angry. Eventually, I sensed I was being followed.

It was Major. He was keeping his distance, like he knew I didn't want company, and he hung his head when I turned around and spotted him on the far side of the road, like he thought he might be in trouble for following me. A car was approaching and I could see him clearly in the car's headlights. We looked into each other's eyes, and when he realized that I wasn't mad at him, his head came up and he started across the road toward me.

"Major! No!" I shouted, but the car was moving fast. The driver hit the brakes, but couldn't stop in time. The car's front bumper caught his hindquarters and he went skidding down the road, struggling and fighting to regain his footing before finally managing to make it to his feet, at which point he took off, running into the field near to where I stood, heading home.

The car stopped, and the driver turned out to be Maquitta, my cousin Nelson's girlfriend. Nelson jumped out of the passenger seat and jogged over to me.

"I'm sorry man. We didn't see him."

"I wasn't trying to tear up my new car," Maquitta added, which infuriated me, and I yelled at them.

When I got back to the house, I called for Major and hunted around outside until I eventually found him. Aside from a couple of scrapes where he'd slid down the road, he seemed to be fine. I suddenly felt guilty, because if I hadn't gone storming off down the road, this wouldn't have happened.

Dad was sitting at the table when I went inside.

"Dad," I said softly, "I'm sorry I flew off the handle earlier—I think the devil got me for cutting up, because Major followed me down the road and got hit by a car." He looked at me, calm but concerned.

"He's ok," I assured him. "But it wouldn't have happened if I hadn't been acting crazy."

He nodded. "I always tell you boys that God don't like ugliness."

Indeed he did. I heard those same words from him so many times over the years, but it really began to sink in that God might punish us for bad actions. At the same time, He also rewards us for good actions and deeds. Even more so, that Major wasn't killed was proof of God's mercy. The next day Major moved a little stiffly, no doubt sore, but acted enough like his old self that we were convinced he would be all right.

Chapter Six

Sometime around the seventh grade I started taking karate lessons with my brother David and a couple of our cousins. My cousin Gregory was our instructor and he seemed to me to be the toughest man on the planet. He would run us until we dropped and make us do stretches that seemed insane, and yet we loved every minute of it. He was home from the service and had spent ten years training in the martial arts in Okinawa, Japan, with true masters. He took our classes very seriously, teaching us Kenpo Karate. Oddly, neither David nor I were getting sick as often as we had before we started these lessons.

After about a year of training, Gregory arranged for all of us to compete in a tournament in Catonsville, Maryland. We climbed into two cars, Eddie driving his car with David, Jeff (one of Eddie's buddies), Jack and myself, while Gregory drove his car accompanied by his sisters Cathy and Tracy. When we stopped along the way to refresh ourselves, David was getting so excited that he started practicing his kicks all over the place. He tried to catch Eddie off guard with a faked kick as a joke, calling Eddie's name. Eddie turned to look at him as he faked a snap kick. But David's shoe flew off and caught Eddie in the eye. So Jeff took the wheel while Eddie rode with his head tilted back, nursing his eye, a cold can of soda serving as a makeshift ice pack.

The tournament was in the Catonsville Community College gymnasium, which was enormous, with people milling about everywhere. I was registered as a white belt, a basic beginner stage, and entered into the kata competition. To my amazement, I tied for first place with a white girl the same size and age as me. We had to perform again for the tiebreaker, and told we would be allowed to choose to repeat our earlier performance or choose a new one. She chose to perform the same kata over again while I chose a different one. I was delighted when I completed it without a single mistake, but, still, they gave first place to her. I couldn't quite figure out why, whether they'd chosen her because she was white or if, perhaps, my having chosen a different routine made it appear that I was too advanced for our category. Nevertheless, I was proud to be bringing home a second-place medal from my very first competition. I stuck with it and by the time I was eighteen, we were all registered in the black belt category. It was a wonderful sense of accomplishment.

I went through school always being considered too small or too frail for just about everything. One other significant issue was that I had a very weak and underdeveloped bladder, so there were times when I found myself at odds with some of the teachers who felt I just wanted to get out of the classroom for a while. Unfortunately, they all learned that I had a real problem at the expense of my embarrassment. One of my seventh-grade teachers decided that he was not going to let me out of his class for bathroom breaks anymore, so when I raised my hand and asked to be excused, he said no. By the end of class I was in tears, because I had wet my pants. After that, the teachers just told me to quietly get up and slip out when I absolutely had to go. My weak bladder plagued and embarrassed me my entire childhood. I was into my late teens before I successfully taught myself to wake myself during the night to overcome bedwetting. If I didn't get up every two hours, all night long, then I would be wet. But I was such a heavy sleeper that it was next to impossible to force myself to get up that frequently. Sometimes, my brothers would deliberately embarrass me by bringing it up in front of our family and friends. I don't think they ever knew how much it hurt me inside. I always tried to play it off, but it left scars in me that I have never forgotten. Still, to this day, I love them and would do anything for them that is humanly possible. I still feel that we have bonds tighter than any other family in the world. And, yes, we have as many issues and differences as any other family in the world. Even now I struggle to write about this personal weakness, but God has called me to be truthful and He gave me this testimony to help and inspire someone else who may have similar sufferings.

I stood about four feet, eight inches tall and weighed probably eighty-five to ninety pounds from the eighth grade to the tenth grade. I was so small that if anyone were to mess with me, someone else would step in to take up for me. I had a friend named Eric and he was huge. In or out of school, he always took the time to talk to me. His favorite joke was to call me Perry Mason and ask when I was going to take his case. Then there were the King brothers. They were not twins that I know of, but were in the same grade together, two years ahead of me, and each seemed strong enough to bench-press a bus. They didn't allow anyone to harass or threaten me. Almost every day we had an afternoon ritual where, passing through the halls between classes, they would lift me with one hand and pin me against the wall as high as they could.

"Collins, anybody bothering you today?"

"No, man," was my typical response. "Just you! Now put me down!" There was never any doubt in my mind that, if I said yes, somebody was going to have a bad day.

Being too small for every sport in which we had a team, I was still very happy to be associated with the teams and allowed to travel with them to games and tournaments. Most of the coaches were too concerned with my health to take a chance on letting me play. In junior high school I became the clock/score keeper, and the stats keeper for basketball and the scorebook keeper for baseball. In senior high, I was the clock/score keeper for both basketball and the boys' soccer teams. I was also the manager/trainer for the girls' softball team. I kept the equipment for them and drilled them with running exercises, as well as overseeing batting and fielding practice.

We always had very good teams and these were very exciting times for me. I give my cousin Gordon the credit for my confidence and desire to continue to always try and improve in the sports scene. He was the best coach I ever had in life and he never settled for anything but our best. I tried out for Little League Baseball one summer and, not expecting too much, I was totally surprised that he actually kept me for his team. I was the tiniest player in the entire league and although I didn't get much time in the field, I was allowed to pinch hit quite often. Cousin Gordon discovered that I had the smallest strike zone of anyone on the team, so when he needed a runner on base, he would call me to the plate as a substitute. I would crouch low, shrinking the size of the strike zone, and as a result, no one was able to pitch successfully against me. I was guaranteed to get a walk every time. Whenever I was at bat I would look to Coach and he would give me the no-swing signal to indicate he wanted me to take the walk.

However, one day we were playing a team where the pitcher threw the same pitch over and over. We were beating them rather handily and so Coach decided to give me some more action. Up to the plate I stepped, once again. I looked to Coach expecting his standard no-swing sign, but to my amazement he gave me the sign to swing away. I focused intently on the pitcher and although the first pitch was a ball, he was throwing so slowly that I could easily track the ball. The next pitch I swung away and hit a line drive right at the second baseman. He caught it relatively easily and I was out, but the thing I remember most was that Coach screamed louder than anyone when the ball came off the bat, and when I turned to trot back to the dugout, he was still jumping up and down. That felt as good as if I had hit the ball out of the park.

I got one more turn at bat that day, and the second time, I hit the ball right back at the pitcher. He missed the catch and I was able to log my first base hit. Coach, Cousin Gordon, was just thrilled and I had a moment that I would remember forever. Thank you, cousin, for helping me to feel confident and capable of succeeding at whatever I put my mind to.

One activity I didn't have much confidence in turned out to be swimming. We were so excited when what was then Maryland State College built a brand-new gym facility with an Olympic-size swimming pool. We would catch rides into town and play in the pool or the gym until they closed for the day and made us leave. The lifeguards would always warn that if someone couldn't swim, not to get caught in the deep end, because if you did, and they had to rescue you, they would put you out immediately.

So, one day, I was playing in the pool and inadvertently ventured too close to the edge of the shallow section. The next I knew, I stepped back and the bottom of the pool just disappeared. I was now literally in over my head. I desperately kicked and splashed in an effort to reach the edge, repeatedly sinking and kicking to come back up. I tried to yell for help but was only able to get out a grunt before I went down again. I frantically kicked to the surface again, but now I had swallowed water and could not cry out. I went down one more time and suddenly felt this calm settle over me as my feet brushed the bottom. I forced myself to open my eyes, searching for the closest edge of the pool, and shoved myself upward from the bottom of the pool in that direction. I was close enough to the edge that I only needed to beat the water about twice with my arms before I could reach the edge and grab hold. Exhausted, I pulled myself up out of the water only to find the lifeguard standing over me, an angry look on his face.

"You ain't got to put me out,' I gasped, coughing, "I'm leaving!"

Struggling to keep a straight face, he watched as I headed straight into the locker room. I dried off, got dressed, and sat in the gym, watching the guys play basketball until the rest of my friends were ready to go home. I didn't think about it then but it had to be God giving me the ability to settle and decide how to get out of the water successfully.

When we were ready to go home, we always headed over to the road that led out of town and toward our neighborhood. We would stand on the corner, by the old laundromat, and wait for cars to come through, in hopes of catching a ride. Almost always, someone would come by and we'd get a lift home without a problem, and most of the time it was cousin Sylvester who would invariably be passing about the time we hit the corner. However, if a ride didn't come along, we had to walk the five miles home. We were always fine until we got to a place we called White Marsh Valley. We were always scared to walk past that area because of the spooky stories always being told about it, and whenever you'd go by there, you'd see gleaming eyes in the moonlight or reflecting the cars' headlights. Sometimes, if we just heard the weeds and tree leaves crackle with movement, we would take off running as fast as we could, and didn't slow down until we were way clear of that place. Thank God we always made it home safely.

Chapter Seven

From junior high through senior high, I had three best friends, and we called ourselves The Fantastic Four. Throughout school, from eighth to twelfth grade, Tammy, Precious, Alex and I were virtually inseparable—we went everywhere together. For a while we were joined by Francine, which made us The Fab Five. We shared everything with one another, including teaching each other how to kiss. There was a short time when Tammy was Alex's sweetheart, and Francine was mine, but kissing was as far as it went for us.

Tammy was often the leader of our little group and she knew how to get the best enjoyment out of anything. She would have us laughing and rolling on the floor with jokes or teasing. If we were going out, she announced the game plan or itinerary. I also had a secret crush on Precious that never came to fruition. She was beautiful and as sweet and soft as cotton candy. When I was fourteen, I had a crisis, one of my episodes, that was extremely severe and I ended up missing school for several weeks, most of which I spent in the hospital before they finally sent me home.

I was feeling a bit better by then, but my mom came home early from work one day, very nervous and concerned. I had to go back to the hospital because the doctor had found a problem. For the first time in my life, my illness had a name: sickle cell anemia, type SS. I had no clue what that meant, but they told us there was no cure and that it would be something that I would have to deal with my entire life. We also learned that this was an ailment that primarily affected black people. Later it was determined that there were some cases with other people of color as well. Being basically a minority disease it was no wonder that it got so little attention and took so long in my life to be diagnosed. The Eastern Shore of Maryland was still rife with racial bias and medical attention for blacks was sorely lacking.

As it happened, it turned out to be a good thing that Mom had to take me back to the hospital, because I abruptly relapsed and was readmitted. I don't know if that was a coincidence or if the stress of learning about my condition was more than I could handle. It was still difficult to describe the pain but it seemed like my body was at war with itself and every beat of my heart was an assault on the rest of the body.

I made it through that episode and eventually returned to school, only to find out that Tammy and Precious had been devastated because they thought I was dying and never coming back. We didn't have any real clear understanding of my situation, but The Fantastic Four was reunited, and off and running again.

Other little romances and courtships sprang up here and there as we grew. I soon found out that we had to be very careful whom we tried to court, because Princess Anne was a tiny little town and we had a huge family. I was head over heels for a pretty little girl named Ashley. We would sit on the phone for an hour, content to just listen to each other breathe. Every once in a while, one of us would break the silence.

"You still there?"

"Yes, I'm still here."

One Friday night I went to town with Mom on our grocery night and who should we meet on the street but Ashley and her mom. Our mothers stood chatting, laughing and joking, while Ashley and I stared at each other in disbelief. How could they possibly know each other? They must have read our minds because all of a sudden Ashley's mom looked at her.

"Is this the Perry you've been spending all that time talking to on my phone? Girl, that's your cousin. You might as well get that out of your head right now."

Ashley cried, "That's not fair!"

Our moms decided right then, between them, that they needed to make sure our families knew who all of their members were!

After that, I had another little sweetheart, called Candy. At the time, it was not uncommon to venture twenty to thirty miles from home on our bikes during the summer. We would take the back roads to Pocomoke City and that was how I met this little cutie, when she was staying in a little house right at the edge of the road we cycled past. In school I used to tiptoe by her classroom door and, making sure to stay out of the teacher's sight, I would get her attention and wink at her. She and the other kids got a real kick out of that. Not far from where she lived was another family that we became great friends with, the Coker family. Mike, Darryl, and I had huge crushes on Sherice, Shawna, and Nicki. To our dismay we heard the same song: "Boy, that's your cousin. You can't be messing with that girl."

Through the years they've all remained great friends and family, and we now have reunions so we don't forget our people, and hopefully so our children will know who their people are and not get tangled up the wrong way.

When I reached sixteen, I guess the hormones just went crazy. From then on, we couldn't wait for Friday and Saturday nights. Karate had really brought Eddie, Jack, and I close as well. Eddie was the oldest, and first to get a car, and soon we were on the hunt for girls. Salisbury was our new stomping grounds, primarily because we would be less likely to inadvertently hit on relatives. Unfortunately, we ran into another little obstacle which put a damper on our activities. The Salisbury boys didn't take too kindly the idea of us outsiders encroaching on their territory.

My brother Kenny was in his senior year and attended the vocational school in Salisbury, and was on the varsity basketball team, which boosted his popularity. One day, one of the Salisbury boys got upset because a little lady he fancied was paying Kenny a little too much attention. Stephon was cautious about approaching Kenny individually, but when he was accompanied by the rest of his crew, he would make challenging remarks. Kenny was a quiet and humble kind of guy who never got into trouble in school, but he was built like a Mack truck. That might explain why Stephon waited until the last day of the vocational school program period to challenge Kenny outright, but his crew dragged him away before it got physical.

Shortly after that, Stephon also got into confrontation with my cousin Jack, where he then, as if the mayor of Salisbury, proclaimed a ban, effective immediately, on any Princess Anne boys from coming into his town. Of course, none of us took him seriously and we all came and went as we pleased.

Then, one weekend, there was a big buzz about a huge house party in Salisbury. They were always fun times for us, because everybody knew everybody and we would laugh and clown around and make passes at the girls. It was just great innocent fun. So, Eddie, his brother Clark, Jack, and I saddled up and rode into town. It turned out to be the largest party I had ever seen in my life. We had to park blocks away and walk back to the house. There were people everywhere and the house was so packed, people couldn't dance or hardly move through the house. Just out of curiosity we decided to circle through and meet back outside. As we squeezed and wormed our way through, the atmosphere changed.

"Stephon", a guy called out. "Hey, where's Stephon? Hey Stephon, you've got company!"

That was my cue to head toward the closest exit, and I took it. When I got outside, I found Eddie already out in the yard, and he and I began to look for Clark and Jack.

Stephon and his crew appeared on the steps of the house, trapping Jack at the door. The yard filled with kids and I found myself separated from Eddie, mobs pressing against each of us, daring us to move. I tried to reason with the guys pressing against me until one guy came straight at me.

"Shut up and don't move!" he barked. He had something in his hand that he was trying to conceal it from me. I watched, frozen, as he moved through the crowd toward Eddie. Another movement by the front door caught my eye and I turned and saw Stephon hit Jack in the face. Jack stumbled down, off the steps. Stephon and his buddies jumped Jack and began beating and kicking him. I felt the group surrounding me press against me more tightly, nudging and pushing me. At that point, I knew we were all going down. I braced myself, only to see two large guys, friends of Eddie, who were wading through the crowd. I watched, astonished, as people were flipped and thrown into the air. The crowd separated, helpless to resist, as if it were Moses parting the Red Sea. The two guys motioned to me.

"Get to the road, Collins," as they pressed on toward Eddie and Jack. I wasted no time and strode toward Eddie's car. Eddie ran toward me, opened the trunk, and yanked out his jack handle.

"They've got weapons," he said, at my horrified look. "I'm going back for Jack."

But before he reached the crowd, Jack appeared and they returned. We got into the car before we realized that Clark was still missing. Eddie drove toward the house and stopped when we spotted Clark heading in our direction. He got into the car. Eddie pulled away and we were headed for home, but Eddie was in excruciating pain. Somebody had hit him in the jaw with something heavy. Jack admitted he might have a broken rib, so we headed for the hospital in Salisbury.

Small towns are small towns, and word quickly spread to Princess Anne that we had been attacked. Without hesitation, my brothers, cousins, and friends converged on Salisbury with a vengeance. The emergency room was awash with patients over the course of that night. Jack, as it turned out, had only bruised his ribs; they weren't broken. Eddie, however, had a broken jaw and had to stay in the hospital for a couple of days. When he came home, his jaw was wired shut. Apparently, the guy who'd ordered me to shut up had a set of brass knuckles concealed in his hand.

Eddie knew who he was and swore that he would catch up to him again.

Meanwhile, over the next week or so, our guys made repeated raids on Salisbury. It seemed like an all-out gang war, which came to a head when our basketball team was competing at one of the Salisbury schools. While the game was underway, someone sliced all four tires of my cousin Josh's car. After the game when the guys came out and found the tires cut, they really went off the deep end. They rounded up enough spare tires to get the car back on the road and proceeded to go straight after Stephon. He must have known something heavy was coming down, because he'd immediately run home after the game. The guys went to his house and knocked on the door. When his mother answered, they walked past her and grabbed him. They threatened to beat him to a pulp unless he paid to replace the cut tires. His mother began crying, pleading with them not to hurt him, and his parents paid them for the tires on the spot. That was the last I ever heard of Stephon. It may be that his parents sent him away to keep him out of trouble.

Eddie finally healed after about six weeks, so the bands and braces were removed and he was his old self again. Shortly afterwards, he was driving his boss's well-drilling rig through Salisbury and happened to spot the guy who had hit him with the brass knuckles. He slammed on the brakes, the guy looked over, and their eyes locked. Eddie's attacker took off, running down the street, and Eddie apparently leaped from the truck before it had even come to a total stop (although he later said it only rolled a few feet further and didn't hit anything). Eddie has always been one of the fastest guys I know, so it's no surprise that he caught the guy and pounded him to the pavement, right on the street. That was the last I heard of any conflicts between the guys from Salisbury and the guys from Princess Anne. I'm sometimes reminded of those brass knuckles and how close I came to being hurt as badly as Eddie, which, in my case, could also have triggered another crisis episode. Again, it was by God's grace that nobody was killed during those crazy, senseless times.

Chapter Eight

Josh, the cousin who got his tires cut that night, had a late model Chevy Malibu. It was a pretty gold tone and he had been building it up with high-performance parts and beautiful deep-dish chrome wheels. It had a four-speed manual shift and we all admired it. After I got my license he taught me how to drive a stick shift. I was so proud to be able to cruise around behind the wheel of such a classy and powerful machine. I was nervous while he was teaching me but he seemed to be very calm and very patient. It's ironic that he and I have had great relationships through all the years and yet we ultimately became fierce competitors through our love of the sport of drag racing. He became legendary, and was invariably mentioned whenever the subject of racing arose during our early years.

After the house party scene played out, we found other adventures to keep us occupied. Eddie bought a beautiful 1972 Charger. It was green with a white vinyl top and had a 400-cubic-inch motor. The car would flat out fly and we never were able to figure out what its top speed was. We began to take rides to Ocean City, Maryland, and cruise the main boulevard, just checking out the scenes. Often we would stop and walk the boardwalk and play some of the games or ride the go-carts. Ocean City is a straight shot down Route 50 from Salisbury. Normally it took about thirty minutes to make the ride, but one night we flew, making it there in about ten minutes, because Eddie and Jack decided they wanted to see how much of the 160-mile-per-hour speedometer they could reach.

At 135 mph, the car changed its sound and became really quiet. The lines on the road closed in up ahead, coming together to a point, and blurred. At 140 mph, Ellis came to his senses and took his foot off the accelerator. I was relieved, to say the least, having been holding my breath the entire time.

We arrived in Ocean City, and while cruising up Ocean Highway we stopped at a red light. A pretty red Charger pulled up alongside, the engine emitting a deep and threatening growl. As we check each other out, the other driver guns the accelerator, issuing the challenge we readily accept.

As the light changes to green, away we both tore. The other Charger initially jumped out ahead of us by a couple of feet, but we rapidly pulled up to where we were neck in neck, before we screamed by him. Our progress was halted by the next red light. He gunned his engine again and we both took off. To our delight, the same thing happened—despite his initial lead, we closed the gap seconds later and left him behind.

At the next light, he conceded and rolled down his window to talk to Eddie.

"Man, what you got in that thing?"

It turned out that his was a 340-cubic-inch engine, no match for our 400ci. He conceded, and we cordially went our separate ways. It was amazing that we didn't cross paths with the police that night, as no doubt we would have been arrested.

We turned our attention to the night-club scene, often frequenting the VFW, the Supper Club, and the Night Shift. In the beginning, I was too young to get in, so I mingled with the crowd of youths who gathered outside. Inside or out, alcohol and the affections of the ladies proved to be a volatile combination. Quite often the evenings would erupt in fistfights merely because somebody's girl looked at someone the wrong way. There were, generally, only two things that spawned fights around the area: girls and drag races. We've always loved cars—it's in our blood. As kids, Mom and Aunt Judy would sometimes challenge each other in the lunch runs to the store. Those big old farm trucks didn't have much high-speed potential but they had fun with them once in a while.

My uncles and older cousins also had the "need for speed" in their veins and gave us our first glimpse of the most popular muscle cars of our era. Quite often we would snap to attention and race toward the road whenever we heard that old familiar growl of a finely tuned V-8 engine, and took pride in being able to identify them before we could see them. There was the '69 Road Runner, the '71 Super Bee, the '66 and '67 Chevelle SS, the '67 and '69, GTO and the '69 Olds 442, to name a few. Uncles Sam and Ricky and cousins Charles, Sonny, Woodson, and Lenwood would light up the road on any given day. I fell head-over-heels in love when Woodson came home from the army sporting a black 442 with white stripes and brilliant white interior. It was the most beautiful sight I had ever seen.

It wasn't long before some of the boys were telling a story of how, on one Sunday, during the local baseball game, Woodson was sitting behind the wheel, parked on the street, and someone walked over and put a beer can down in front of the right front tire and bet that he couldn't jump it. Woodson smiled.

The Olds had Mickey Thompson Street tires on the back that were about twenty-four inches wide, on chrome deep-dish rims. When he revved up the four-speed big block and cut loose, the front wheel totally cleared the can. Instantly Woodson's car became a legend.

One day we heard the familiar roar of competing engines and tore out of the house in time to see Woodson and Lenwood coming around the bend, head to head. Lenwood's GTO was on the inside lane and Woodson's 442 on the outside. Woodson's tires slipped off the shoulder as he raced around the curve and he lost control. The car hurtled around the bend sideways and made a beeline for our driveway. The rear of the car slammed into our mailbox and was propelled back across the road, narrowly missing the back end of Lenwood's GTO. The 442 hit the ditch, launched high into the air, and came down flat on its top in the field opposite, as we watched in horror. When it hit the ground, it sounded like a bomb going off, all of the glass in the car exploding on impact.

I don't know what was more shocking, what we'd just witnessed or the fact that Woodson crawled out of the car, unscathed. He never said a word, just stood there looking at what was left of his pride and joy, and scratching his head. He turned and walked home and returned shortly with his tractor. He tied a chain to the car and flipped it back onto its wheels, then hitched it up, and towed it home.

Chapter Eight

His heart must have been as broken as our mailbox, which we eventually located about a hundred yards down the road, near Mr. Theodore's house. It took ages but, eventually, the 442 was fixed and back on the road, looking astonishingly good as ever. It made such a strong impression on me that two of my first three cars were '69 Olds Cutlasses. I couldn't afford a 442 model, but I still tried to soup them up as much as I could.

My cousin Charles, who lived in Suffolk but frequently traveled back to our area, which was truly home to him, had his own business restoring classic cars and he owned quite a collection of immaculate Mopar beauties. Among them was a beautiful '67 Plymouth Belvedere dubbed "The Right One". He kept its virtual twin, a Dodge Coronet, with forest green paint and red stripe molding, looking just as clean and beautiful. The body style and paint made it difficult to tell them apart with the exception of the name engraved on both doors of the Belvedere. The difference between them was staggering, however, if you picked the Plymouth "Right One" to race. The Belvedere was a full-body, showroom-condition, screamer of a race car. The only thing not factory looking about it was the built-in roll cage and a monster 440-cubic-inch motor capable of running ten seconds through the quarter-mile all day long. We would get so excited seeing him ride past on any given weekend with The Right One towed behind him. He would always stop by our house either Saturday or Sunday and we couldn't wait to get to the track on Sunday and watch them go to work.

Charles was the coolest man I have ever seen behind the wheel of a race car. He was also the smartest. Everyone on the race scene seemed bent on showing how fast they could go, and that often resulted in blown engines and inconsistent times. Charles tuned, timed, and studied the Belvedere until he could set his throttle to run the same time over and over again. The car was capable of breaking out of the ten-second bracket if he wanted it to, but he kept it dialed back so that all he had to worry about was getting traction and his reaction time. He became an absolute perfectionist at handling the car. They were like one with each other, and together they really were The Right One.

We watched as he won events time after time, and it became obvious after a while that the good ole boy network was not thrilled with his continued success. They began to switch and shift cars in the lanes to try and line up their best, to eliminate him early. They soon found out that he was still knocking out all of their favorites, so on other Sundays, they started shuffling the cars to avoid him knocking out their favorites too early. They hoped that, by the end of the day, somebody would eliminate him or just maybe he would break the car or slip up and lose on his own.

No matter what they tried, he always finished the day somewhere near the top. I observed him take the entire day to the number one spot on two occasions and it was the most thrilling time at the track that I have ever had in my life. Charles has been a legend in my eyes and our family's own personal hero. He taught us in so many ways what it takes to be a champion and how we must strive to be the best we can be in all that we endeavor to do. Our love of cars and appreciation for the art of restoration is totally wrapped up in the accomplishments of Cousin Charles.

Chapter Nine

My dad came home one day with a Plymouth Fury and it turned out to be what was referred to in those days as a police interceptor, meaning it was designed to be a sleeper, a well-disguised police tool for chasing down those hard to catch lawbreakers. Its looks were unassuming but the investment was in the 383-cubic-inch motor, which packed a serious punch.

The first day Dad brought it home, he had to go back to town for something. When he pulled out of the yard, he decided to show off a little bit and stepped down on the gas hard. The car immediately spun around in the road and started back into the driveway. It scared Dad so badly that he went to town and had the mechanic turn the carburetor and the timing down, afraid that if any of his boys drove it, someone might get hurt. (I don't know where he could have gotten that idea...)

Nonetheless, the car was still plenty fast and soon gained a reputation around town. We periodically got a chuckle out of riding with Dad only to have someone pull up beside him and gun their engine in an attempt to challenge him to a race. Dad, baffled by this, would just look over at them and tell us they were crazy. He may have eventually figured out what was happening, but my younger brothers and I were not about to explain it to him—or how we knew what was going on.

In 1974 my brother Calvin, aka Moon, bought a beautiful brand-new AMC Javelin—spotless, mean, and downright sexy. It was green, with wide gold stripes and deep-dish chrome wheels, and sparkled, reflecting the sun's rays, to where you couldn't keep your eyes off it, grinning as you watched until it disappeared down the street. Was it fast! He got challenges to race everywhere he went, and I can't recall any races where he came out on the bottom in those days.

Equally as passionate as my love for cars was my love for the ladies. Quite often the cars would be the first thing to draw the attention of the ladies, so we kept them clean and sexy-looking. My brothers and I became very popular with the ladies and, as I said before, nothing sparked a fight quicker than girls and drag races, so we had more than our fair share of late-night brawls.

By the time I reached the age of seventeen, my brothers Larry and Kenneth had enlisted in the armed services. Larry joined the Marines and Kenny the Air Force. When they came home on leave, they were truly lean, mean, fighting machines. Larry was the leanest and the meanest, even as a young kid, and now the Marines had taught him that one man could beat ten. He lived and breathed that philosophy, so if someone said, "Fight," he just started swinging.

One night, as we sat in a club, a scene began to brew between Kenny and another guy because of a young lady he had become acquainted with. The guy was her ex-boyfriend, but he refused to leave her alone and was trying to dominate her by making her afraid. Kenny decided not to have it out with him, so we prepared

Chapter Nine

to leave, but the thugs he was with were itching for trouble. They followed us out into the parking lot, cursing and making threats. By that time, our patience had pretty much expired, so my four brothers and I gathered into a tight group and the battle line was drawn. Once we gathered in like that, anyone who approached us was bound to get flattened. They all stood back and kept their distance, just verbally taunting us, until one of them declared that he wasn't scared and made the colossal mistake of walking straight up to Larry, the one least likely to show him any mercy. Larry's hands were at his sides, and he warned the guy to stay back, but the guy kept coming.

Before he could react, Larry cold-cocked him with one punch and then proceeded to revive him by shoving his head into a water puddle. But when he failed to let the guy come up for air, we were forced to pull him off and hold him back. No one else made a move. In answer to our challenging looks, they began to disperse.

Larry looked down at his hand. It was pretty obvious that he'd broken it, so I drove him to the hospital. He wore a cast for six weeks and as soon as it was removed, he broke it again on somebody else's face. It's a good thing he never hit anyone with the cast or we might have been looking at a homicide.

Larry and Kenny also came home with new choices of transportation. Larry bought a '73 Javelin and Kenny was sporting a '72 Dodge Dart, built up for serious business. They soon had their own reputations as not so good candidates for challenges. By now everyone was getting into modifying the engines of their hotrods. The high-lift cams, Hooker headers, and Harley carburetors were in full demand and the competition was getting pretty steep.

By now I was a high school senior and I had begun to build a rather steady relationship with a young lady named Sasha. Unfortunately, there were some rumors of other guys still pushing for her attention that kept us from becoming totally exclusive with one another. Even so, she was a pretty, little skinny girl who always lit up my life whenever she came to find me. We had the strongest physical attraction for each other right from the beginning. It was more than anything I had ever previously experienced. We could be mad at each other one minute and pulling each other's clothes off the next. There was no match for our sexual attraction for one another.

However, I soon learned that sex was another potential trigger for the dreaded sickle-cell crisis. It usually depended on how tired or stressed I was, but there were more than a few times that the throbbing pain would rapidly build in my chest or legs. Sasha had gotten really good at recognizing the signs and she would rush to get me home so I could climb into bed to wait it out. Sometimes the pains subsided by the next day, but sometimes they wouldn't and I would be off to the hospital again. We always kept those episodes between the two of us and made up something to tell the family. She always found lots of time to come and visit me when I was bedridden.

The Fantastic Four was still on a roll in school and all too soon it was time to start thinking about our prom arrangements. Alex and Tammy had dates already, but Precious did not, so we started brainstorming how to get her a date. The problem was that her mom was very strict and wouldn't let her go out with hardly anyone. She already knew and liked us as Precious' friends, so we decided that I should be her date and I would break off my

Chapter Nine

relationship with Sasha so I wouldn't have to worry about a conflict. Thinking about it later, it seemed a rather underhanded thing to do, and I felt badly, but as it turned out, her old flame had come home from the army and she wasn't missing me much at all.

The prom was nice and everyone had a good time. We rode around from place to place for a little while afterward, but I had been warned by Precious' mom that if she wasn't home by midnight, she would be on the phone to the police. So, when everyone began to split off in pairs, I pointed the car straight for her house. We arrived right around midnight to find her mom standing in the doorway, arms folded, toes tapping impatiently. I walked her to the door and said good night to them both. Unable to catch up with any of the crew at that point, I called it a night and went home.

After the prom, our attention was turned to graduation and the excitement was mounting rapidly. Our cousin Sherice was elected class president, and we spent "Senior Hook Day," as a great day, in the park. We laughed, teased and played the whole day. When it was over, we began to worry about the repercussions of skipping school, both about what the school officials would do as well as our parents. Some of us were lucky enough to have our parents vouch for our absence, because the school threatened to ban us from marching at our graduation. The graduation exercise was short, sweet, and classy, and I don't recall any of us not being allowed to march.

Chapter Ten

Summer was now in full swing and once again the ball games were rolling; the days were spent working to earn money and the nights out on the town were tremendous. Weekend street races were now a ritual. My brothers had their own muscle cars and were becoming quite renowned. My brother Michael had joined the pack by now with a Chevy Nova. It was rather plain-looking and unassuming, but we soon learned what a hidden treasure the original small-block 400-cubic-inch Chevy motor was. The thing had so much torque that it rode down the street looking slightly shifted and twisted. We joked on a regular basis about it doing the "crab walk." Overall, it provided a ton of fun and enjoyment as we watched it leap off the line and fade away from the competition.

My summer took on a different turn around the Fourth of July, when Sasha returned to rekindle our relationship. We hadn't spoken since March, but the chemistry was still there. We went to a movie that night and afterward we officially made up.

A couple of months later, the evidence of that night became apparent. We had a baby on the way, and rumors began to fly about whether or not I was actually the father. It seems everyone I knew had some sort of opinion about our relationship and,

Chapter Ten

consequently, I always had this dark cloud of doubt hanging over my head. I think that, in many ways, this was an insurmountable obstacle to the chances of the two of us ever becoming a successful couple.

I started my first semester of college in the fall and it was pretty interesting. Maryland State College was now called The University of Maryland Eastern Shore, and was only four or five miles from home. That was where, as kids, we used to hitch rides back and forth just to spend time at the swimming pool and I'd nearly drowned.

It felt great to be a college student and I decided to study electrical engineering. Kenny decided to leave his car home when he returned to the base and gave me permission to drive it to the campus for classes. It was powerful and the high-lift cam made it rock when idling. The students would all turn and watch as I pulled up to park or cranked up to leave. I loved the heavy growl and the feeling of raw power in my hands, but I resisted the temptation of showing off.

February proved to be a bit rough weather-wise, and the Dart did not like wet or freezing conditions. As I came home and turned onto our road one afternoon, the car began to slide as I approached the American Legion. When I tapped the brakes, the car went into a full 360-degree spin and landed in the ditch. One of the guys in the neighborhood was passing by and stopped to give me a hand. He hooked his truck up to the car with a chain and was able to pull it out. There was now a dent in the rear right fender but, otherwise, it looked ok. That evening one of my brothers called Kenny and told him what happened before I'd had the chance. When I explained what had happened, he didn't sound too upset, but he told me not to take it out anymore. So now I was forced to catch rides to town or use Mom and Dad's car when it was available.

Time seemed to literally fly during this time, and before I knew it, it was mid-March and I got word that Sasha was in the hospital, about to deliver. By the time I was about to start my geometry class, I found I could no longer concentrate, so I asked my instructor if he would excuse me from class because I needed to get to the hospital. He wasn't as enthusiastic as I was, but he excused me.

Tina was born about an hour after I arrived at the hospital and she was just perfect. We bonded immediately, and as time went by, she wouldn't tolerate anyone handling her, except her mom, her maternal grandmother, and me, and if anyone else tried, her screams quickly put an end to it and they would retreat.

Sasha worked at the hospital in Salisbury, so when it came time for her to return to work that summer, I kept Tina most of the time and that strengthened our bond. As fate would have it, Tina was born on March 17, so she shared a birthday with my late sister Margaret. As I was on break from school then, it was convenient for me to watch over Tina, but I hadn't yet paid for the past year's tuition and discovered that I couldn't receive my grades or return to school the following semester until I paid up. That meant I was forced to go out and get a job to pay for school. It also meant that I could no longer keep Tina while her mom worked. Fortunately, Sasha's mother and grandmother were able to step in and help, so Tina was in very good hands.

My sister Vernetta and her husband Cornelius sold me their '69 Cutlass for $200, so now I had my first car. I got a job working for Somerset County as a carpenter's apprentice, painting and doing minor repairs on various county buildings. It was a pretty easygoing appointment, until January rolled around and I found myself working outside in the cold at a migrant workers' camp. A few of us were assigned to dig a trench and the ground was so hard, we had to use picks as well as shovels. After a couple of days of that intense hard labor, I started to feel poorly. By that evening, I was experiencing waves of sharp pains that were building faster and more intensely than I had experienced in a long time. Before the evening was over, Mom and Dad bundled me up and we headed for the hospital. From mid-January through February, I was in the hospital, and for most of that period I was being given injections in my butt around the clock, every four hours—so, six times a day, seven days a week, for about six weeks. There was a blizzard in February which I never witnessed, and when I finally was released from the hospital I was amazed by all of the mountains of snow that had been plowed into the corners of all the parking lots.

It was apparent that I couldn't continue working outside in the wintertime. My mom and my sister Belinda had decided to job hunt for me while I was still in the hospital. Belinda called to say there was a position open at Goddard Space Flight Center, on Maryland's Western Shore, which was being vacated by my brother Michael, who had scored a higher-paying job as a driver for UPS, and she wanted me to come up and apply for it. So, I packed a bag, drove to Belinda's house, and applied for the job. Everyone there had been so pleased with the job that Michael had done that they were very open to the idea of hiring his brother.

So, on March 12, 1979, I started my first professional position as a data clerk with MATSCO, a subsidiary of General Electric

Co., and was assigned to the Nimbus Operations Control Center. It was agreed that I would live with Belinda, and sleep on her couch.

Nimbus was an Earth Observatory Satellite with several interesting instruments on board. I arrived during the heyday of Nimbus 7, which was the last of the Nimbus series. We collected data from various instruments, which included the Total Ozone Mapping Spectrometer(TOMS), the Solar Backscatter for the Ultra Violet(SBUV), among others. I collected the data through printouts and real-time data sheets and delivered them to various scientists around the center. It was a wonderful position and the first time I had ever started a job where I made more than minimum wage.

My boss, Benny, was great in every sense of the word. He was smart and knew every aspect and detail of the Nimbus Satellites, from start to finish. I learned what the term "being a professional" really meant. You were expected to do your job to the fullest, with little or no supervision. As long as you got your job done in a timely and efficient manner, no one would be breathing down your neck or harassing you about your comings and goings. I was working with a great team, which consisted of satellite operations supervisors, evaluators, system analysts, and mission planners. All of them pitched in to teach me day-to-day operations from their perspectives and I learned more from them than a four-year degree would have given me.

They taught me how to send commands to the satellite, how to read the data that was being downloaded, and how to plot and coordinate the passes that the "bird" took on a daily basis with the various tracking stations. The guys were extremely technical, but very much a bunch of jokers as well. They were always finding

Chapter Ten

ways to tease me, having discovered just how gullible I could be. I was an old country boy getting schooled by my city-slicker comrades, and I loved every minute of it. We felt like family and I came to love Bob, Seechuk, Berry, Ed, Joe, and Walt like brothers. Robert Berry and Ed Rutkowski became like father figures over time. If I ever had a problem, personal or otherwise, they were always willing to listen or assist.

Berry was the only other black guy in the group. He was a minister and as big a jokester as the rest. I visited his home on many occasions and they would always feed me. One day after I worked on his car, they gave me dinner. It was the first time I'd ever had eggplant parmesan and I loved it so much, I would always request it whenever he wanted to treat me. I lovingly gave it the name "The Berrino Special." That particular evening, I accidentally left behind my jacket when I left for home. The next morning, at work, Berry came to me with this very stern look on his face and demanded to know why he'd found my jacket in his bedroom. He also wanted to know why his wife knew exactly where it was. My jaw dropped. I looked around to see all of the guys standing there, staring at me. I was so stunned, so caught off guard that I couldn't think of a word to say. Everyone abruptly burst into laughter at my shocked expression. I was so embarrassed that he'd got me so good. Berry's wife Natalie was admittedly an extremely attractive lady, but they were a loving and hospitable family, and we kept in touch for years after I left Nimbus.

Having found that I knew a lot about cars, Berry wasn't the only one who paid me to work on theirs. Sometimes I would spend my lunchtime installing brake pads or changing sparkplugs. For larger jobs, like complete tune-ups and alternator replacements,

I would visit my co-workers' homes after work or on weekends. Goddard Space Flight Center turned out to be not just a base but a very close-knit community. The Control Center I worked in was run by MATSCO and GE, but the Operations and Data Processing Center attached to us was run by Bendix Field Engineering Corporation, or BFEC, and I was surprised to see that the employees were predominantly black. Over time I learned that our side consisted of more highly paid employees, although I was the least paid among both sides. Data clerk was the most junior of all of the positions, but I was happy because the job was more exciting and better paid than any other job that I had held.

Once in a while, however, the real world would creep in, a reality check that prejudice was still alive and well. For example, there was one guy that I would pass in the hallway about the same time every morning. I would smile and say, "Good morning," and never once did he acknowledge my existence. I made it a point to greet him with a smile every day for months, until one day I stopped seeing him. He must have either changed his schedule or got another job. It wouldn't be the last time I would encounter someone who didn't see me as worthy of merely muttering the words "good morning."

Because of our sickle cell disease, my brother David and I were enrolled in a study at the Howard University Hospital Clinic, in D.C., when I was about seventeen, where Mom and Dad would bring us about once a month. The doctors always questioned our mom as to how she was raising us, because our bodies were more developed and we appeared overall healthier and stronger than other patients in the study. Mom told them that we ate like horses when we felt good, but that she never coddled us or stopped us from doing anything the rest of our brothers did.

Dr. Castro was the most renowned physician and foremost authority on sickle cell disease in the country. He was always on point when it came to treating us. His staff ran the clinic and it was a smooth and timely operation. We got to know other patients like us, along with many of the hospital staff.

Now that I was living and working on Maryland's Western Shore, I was closer to the clinic and could take myself to my appointments. I had become a responsible adult. After a few years, the clinic was being run by an attractive female doctor whom I'd developed a little crush on. I always got nervous when she decided to do a full assessment of our conditions, which included blood work and a complete physical exam. It was nerve racking to have her examining my private parts.

The biggest advantage of participating in the study was that we always got great treatment whenever a crisis came on and we had to be hospitalized. I never had to worry about staff who didn't know me looking at me like I was some drug addict looking for a fix. Out of all the hospitals I've stayed in, Howard University was the tops (with the exception of a couple of incidents I would experience a few years down the road, on which I'll elaborate later).

In the meantime, I headed home every weekend, when I wasn't working on someone's car, for two days of nonstop fun and extracurricular activities. Our buddy Lee was stationed at Andrews Air Force Base and we would take either his car or mine. He had a beautiful '72 Mustang that was the Ford classic light blue. He would pick me up, hand me the keys, and sit back with a beer in hand and enjoy the ride. Ironically, after all the trips we made back and forth to the Eastern Shore, I ended up cracking up his prized possession on a simple Saturday night run to the store. As I was leaving Mom and Dad's, Kenny, who had borrowed Vernetta and Cornelius's Plymouth Arrow, said he would follow on behind me.

All the way down the road I kept looking in the rearview mirror for his headlights, but there was no sign of him. When I got to the American Legion, I decided to pull over and wait for him. There were lots of people there and the lot was almost full. After a few minutes, as I sat there looking down the road, I could make out the glow of lights. As the lights got closer, I could tell they were that of the Arrow. I decided to pull back out ahead of him to continue on, now that he was close enough to see me. What I didn't realize was that, having expected me to be already in town, he was speeding, trying to catch up. I pulled out into the street and didn't notice that the distance between our two cars had closed way too quickly until it was too late.

Kenny slammed on his brakes and I swerved to get off the road as fast as I could, but it was too late. His rear fender collided with my quarter panel and he bounced off, causing Vernetta's Arrow to spin around 180 degrees.

I got out to assess the damage. The dent in Lee's quarter panel was ugly, but the poor Arrow had the entire rear bumper ripped off. All I could think about was how devastated Lee was going to be. I knew the car was his pride and joy and I was devastated myself to see it damaged. When Lee got there, he was really upset, and all I could do was cry. He cried and yelled, both of us just in pieces.

Finally, after he calmed down, he hugged me and told me it would be ok.

"We can fix this," he said. "Don't worry about it."

He climbed in behind the wheel and headed into town, while I climbed into the Arrow with Vernetta and Kenny and returned home. I can't remember what the reason was why I was headed to town that evening, but obviously, I never did get it done that night. Lee and Vernetta got their cars fixed and soon the incident was forgotten, and Lee and I continued to make our weekend runs back home every Friday after work.

Chapter Eleven

Friday nights when I would arrive, there was inevitably some club or a dance at the school to go to. Saturday would be street races, day and night, plus some fun in the club. Sasha and Tina were always somewhere in the mix, although looking back, I'm ashamed to admit I didn't spend as much time with Tina as I should have, as her father.

Sunday was an all-day outing at the racetrack, followed by a late-night return to Laurel, where Belinda lived. Sometimes I would be so tired, I could barely keep my eyes open. It was then I sensed that God was really looking out for me. One night, at about 1:00 a.m., I was on the road and got as far as Vienna when I drifted off for a moment. When I awoke, I was in the next town, Cambridge, approaching a red light, with a tractor-trailer stopped in front of me.

"Jesus!" I cried, and yanked the wheel to the left. The car screeched into the left lane, missing the truck by maybe a foot. Fortunately, there was no other traffic. As I fought to gain control of the car, it skidded sideways, first in one direction and then the other. Finally, it spun all the way around and came to a stop with the back end peeking into the intersection. I was so close to the

Chapter Eleven

front end of the truck that I could literally reach out my window and touch its front tire. The driver of the truck stared down at me in disbelief. I immediately pulled into a parking lot on the corner and sat there for about thirty minutes, collecting myself and thanking my Maker for sparing my life. I recalled horror stories of people being decapitated after getting wedged under a tractor-trailer and knew I had just escaped death in a most dramatic fashion.

Jesus was there and He answered my cry.

After about a year my cousin Josh came up from home, and he and I decided to get an apartment together. A few months earlier though, before I moved from Belinda's, I became friendly with a sweet, pretty little lady named Katrina. She was young and off limits, but she would always stop by to chat and bombard me with questions about my car and what I was doing when I was working on it. She learned the names and functions of items like a carburetor, distributor, valve cover, and radiator, and I was amazed that she seemed genuinely interested in whatever I was doing. Our attraction to one another grew, even though she knew I had a girl and a daughter who periodically visited me on weekends. Sasha and Tina would catch the Trailways bus to Baltimore and I would pick them up. We would hang out for the weekend, eating, watching TV, and catching up when possible on our lovemaking. But the distance between us proved to be too much and we began to drift apart. I believe we were both to blame for the final breakup but it was a slow and painful process. For me, the deciding moment was when Katrina stepped forward to say she wanted a relationship with me.

When I moved with Josh, we often had brothers and cousins invade our place for weeks at a time. Many of the guys from home got their start camping out at our place. Over the years my brothers Darryl and Kenny, Josh's brother Victor, and cousins Rusty, Mason, Henry, Irvin, Brice, Alex, Nelson, and friend Lee all spent time hanging out with us. In later years, cousins Jason and Thomas (aka Baby Tommy) also hooked up with us. We worked, we drank, we played basketball and sometimes softball. Last, but not least, we chased the ladies. All in all, there were few dull moments.

This was a tumultuous period, as my brothers and cousins entered into a family dispute with my uncles. Darryl and Victor were living with Josh and me at this time and they got jobs selling a variety of goods, from framed pictures and drinking glasses to knife sets, for a popular company. The company kept a record of all of the products they were entrusted with, and anything not accounted for had to come out of their pockets.

On our usual weekend run back home, we made a stop at our uncle's house, and the guys showed everyone there the merchandise they had for sale. Over the course of the visit, however, a coupe items went missing. Naturally, Darryl and Victor got upset when everyone denied any knowledge of where they'd disappeared to, knowing they'd have to cover the cost. Tempers flared, Josh and a couple of my brothers got involved, and the situation rapidly spiraled out of control. A friend of my uncle's, who was there as well, started threatening to shoot somebody. Victor and Josh stormed out, threatening to return with a gun, and then somebody called the police and described Victor and Josh, saying they were carrying a gun and looking for trouble.

Sure enough, the police pulled them over just a couple of blocks from the house, searched the vehicle, found the gun, and arrested them. Upon learning this, my brother Larry, a sergeant

Chapter Eleven

in the Marines, headed home to get his rifle. My mom intercepted him and demanded to know what was going on. He told her about the guy at our uncle's house, waving around a pistol and threatening us. Mom pleaded with Larry not to take the rifle, knowing full well he was capable of using it and eventually he flung it away in frustration, breaking several shingles on the siding of the house.

Mom jumped into her car and hurried over to her brother's house and told all of her boys to go home. Meanwhile, we had discovered that Darryl had also been named as an armed trespasser. Mom headed over to the station and vigorously assured the police that all of her boys were home, at her house, that none of them were armed, and that none of us had any intention of ever returning to our uncle's property. It would be some time before we forgave our uncles, but neither Josh nor his brother Victor, having gotten into serious trouble with the law as a result, never did. Josh was not the same for a long time after the incident, and ultimately left his job and returned to the Shore.

This was also a period of great loss in our family. I came home one weekend and on the Sunday morning, I decided to install new brakes before heading back across the bridge.

The phone rang and it was Nelson.

"Man, come and get me," he said. "I'm going back with you today."

I told him that I had the wheels off at the moment but I'd come and get him as soon as I was done.

"Oh, don't worry about it, then" he assured me. "I'll catch a ride out there to you instead."

As it turned out, he caught a ride into town and then borrowed a friend's motorcycle, bringing along a friend for company, a woman who was about seven or eight months pregnant. But he lost control of the motorcycle, rounding a big curve. The cycle went down into the ditch and hit a concrete piling, at which point Nelson and his friend went flying through the air. Nelson collided with a diamond-shaped reflector sign, which tore him open, and slammed him into the ditch, killing him instantly. His pregnant friend flew off the back and into the woods, bouncing off trees. Her stomach was ripped open, exposing and killing the baby. When the paramedics arrived, they managed to revive her a couple of times and had her air-lifted to the hospital, but she died before they reached the hospital.

Three precious lives were gone so swiftly. It was devastating. Nelson's sister Deneen rode down to the scene with me, and we hugged and cried uncontrollably. She and I had also been close, but this marked the start of a particularly strong connection, and to this day our hearts leap for joy whenever we see each other, having developed a special appreciation of just how quickly life can change.

I found the funeral almost unbearable, and I was gasping for air as I walked toward the car. I had a pain in my heart, but I thank God it didn't turn out to be a full-fledged crisis. I could hear Nelson's voice and kept thinking of his countless pranks and jokes as we left the gravesite. The first few years after his passing, I couldn't maintain composure whenever I heard "It's So Hard to Say Goodbye to Yesterday," by G. C. Cameron. Even now, after more than thirty years, when I hear the song I still think of Nelson. He is forever in my heart.

Chapter Twelve

※

The next divine intervention I experienced occurred one Friday afternoon after we loaded up a couple of our rides to head home for the weekend. My Cutlass, it turned out, had a cracked frame and just as we were coming off the Bay Bridge, the crack fractured and the steering box tore away from the steering column. Here I was, on the bridge, holding onto a steering wheel that had no control over the vehicle. I took my foot off the gas and looked over at Irvin, who was sitting in the passenger seat.

"Man, I just lost my steering!" I gasped.

Irvin went into a panic.

"Man, you got it? Do you got it?" he kept repeating.

"No! Lord Jesus, no," was all I could say.

The car slowed to around thirty miles per hour and as we reached the end of the bridge began to drift casually toward the shoulder on its own accord, as if I were steering and in control. If I had spun the wheel around ten times, it wouldn't have made a difference. When the car reached the shoulder, I hit the brakes and we jerked to a stop.

"Thank you, Lord," I whispered shakily.

We got out and looked under the hood to see if we could figure out what had gone wrong and saw that the steering had completely severed from the vehicle. We called home to ask my brother to bring a trailer to collect the car. My beloved Olds never saw road action again.

Yet, by God's grace, we were safe.

At work I became friends with many of the guys on the BFEC (Bendix Field Engineering Corp.) side and we would get together and hang out at parties and night clubs. Initially I got to know Patrice, Felecia, Henry, and Porche, after which came Larry, Cherice, Benita, Rebecca, and Vanessa. The turnover on that side of the facility was pretty frequent, and eventually Larry, Cherice, and Vanessa became my best friends, and Benita and Rebecca joined us as we expanded into the sports scene, assembling the best volleyball team around the area. Percy, also on our team, was the most feared spiker in the entire county. Porche and Benita were fearless at digging and saving spikes coming from the other side, and I became known as the little guy with the vertical leap. Guys with six to twelve inches over me in height got a rude awakening when their spike got stuffed back at them. We held the number one spot for many years in the Goddard league and one year we became champions of the AAA county league. I later played in a Catholic Church league with a couple of the guys in my control center. There we also won first place one year.

In spite of my bouts with illness, I just loved sports and would risk those episodes for the thrill of the game. By this stage, though, I found myself dealing with an added complication: double pneumonia, caused by fluid buildup in and around both of my lungs. I suspect this condition mostly stemmed from my work environment, because the computer rooms were thermostatically controlled by chilled air that was piped in to keep the hardware cool and functioning. Working in that artificially cool environment and then walking out into really hot and humid weather may have been what increased my risk of developing this condition, known as sickle cell chest syndrome.

During one of these hospitalizations, I encountered a doctor that I had never met before, and after that experience, I prayed that I would never meet him again. He came to get me during the night to remove some of the fluid that had accumulated in my chest cavity. He took x-rays of my chest and then had me to sit in a chair facing its back and hug the back rails. He gave me a couple of injections which he said were to numb my upper back, behind my lungs, and then I saw him hold up an immense needle, one that looked to me to be about a foot long. I felt nothing initially, as he inserted it into my back, but then I felt such intense pain that I thought I was going to die. I screamed as he pushed it deeper and deeper into my chest cavity and began to extract fluid surrounding one of my lungs. I was crying as he pulled it out, not yet realizing that he was about to repeat the process on the other side. I wept, holding on to the chair rails. The second attempt didn't yield as much fluid, but it was sufficient to make him stop, and I was returned to my room, still shaking from the experience.

When he returned to say he needed to perform the procedure again, I flat out refused.

"I will never let you do that to me again, ever," I told him fiercely.

He was taken aback, insisting and trying to strong-arm me, but he knew I meant it when I said no. He left and I never saw or heard from him again. I had had this syndrome six times in my ten years with the Nimbus project, and this was the only time this procedure had been performed. I learned later that the chest Syndrome often resulted in scar tissue building up around the lungs and my breathing capacity was somewhat diminished afterward. This could have been what he was trying to prevent, but all I could think was that there had to be a better way.

A friend of mine, Bob, who also proved to be a great Christian brother, sold me his '71 Mustang Grande when he found out I no longer had a car. It was exceptionally clean inside, although the blue exterior paint had faded somewhat. It was tight, a dream to drive, and handled like a gem. Although the 302-cubic-inch V8 engine was small, I dressed it up to look sportier. I swapped the 2-barrel carburetor for a 4-barrel, which lent it a nice kick, but I didn't try to race it. I just played around with it a little bit from time to time.

One day I came across a guy who was selling an authentic Ram Air hood, and I just had to have it. I paid $100 for it and painted it flat black. Now, with Cragar mag wheels, she had the look of a lean, mean, racing machine. The car was so solid and dependable that I fell totally in love with it. We took many trips back and forth to the Shore. Still, my love for the old Cutlass never died, and when I came upon another '69 Cutlass, in Laurel, that was for sale at a reasonable price, having made sure the body and frame were in good condition, I bought it.

The paint was an ugly chocolate color, so I got my cousin Karol to paint it the same color as my first one. He did a magnificent job and the car became a real head turner for a while. I installed a new sound system in it that was so tight. It was a new generation system from **KRACO** called the Super Sound

Chapter Twelve

Boomers, and featured its own built-in power booster that really caused the car to rock.

Mason and I would ride out in it and check out the ladies, going on a few double dates or just hanging out to see what mischief we could get into. I would ride out to North Lake Park, in Salisbury, on the weekends and we would raise the trunk and blast the latest jams. It sounded like a real DJ out there, with a powerful setup. I used to get Eddie to make me new tapes so I always had something fresh to blast out. You could hear it all over the park, and people would come to hang out, dance, drink, and party down.

Since Josh had returned home, Mason and I were partners in the apartment rental, and we took care of the bills while the other guys came and went, making their new starts in life. Some of them would pitch in when they got a solid job, and we all enjoyed the benefits of having a little more cash on hand to do more of the things we liked.

We would get together in the evenings and play basketball in the gym, until closing time. Guys would come from Bowie and Fort Meade to play us in pick-up games, but they didn't get the best of us very often, because our group was tight and we knew each other's habits and skills. Kenny, Irvin, and Victor had played varsity ball in school, and Mason was shooting three-pointers before there was any such thing. The boy could just throw up long bombs and you'd hear nothing but net. After the games we'd put our money together and buy two or three cases of beer and head back to our crib and party a while.

We usually ate pretty heavily, although not so nutritionally, because Mom would get Swanson microwave dinners by the case and Mason loved to hunt, so he would come back during deer season with more venison than we knew what to do with. We fried it, roasted it, barbequed it, and stewed it in gravy. We cooked deer meat every way we could think of. We ate so much venison that I started acting wild in my sleep. I would wake up with all the covers kicked off the bed or I'd be turned all the way around and be hanging off the foot of the bed. These were wild and crazy times and I'm happy to say that the guys went on to great lives and successful careers. We only lost Nelson to tragedy and the rest of the guys all seemed to find their way to full, meaningful adulthood.

Chapter Thirteen

※

After a couple of years, a new encounter with divine intervention occurred. I was at work when I suddenly became aware of the old familiar dull thud in my chest. As it sharpened, I took two Tylenol and told the guys I didn't feel well and needed to go back home. I made it as far as Laurel and was on a back road called Brock Bridge Road, which ran alongside a small airport, and I remember watching a plane approaching as I passed by.

At the next curve, I must have passed out, because I found myself up the side of the embankment, my Mustang in the midst of a scary rollover.

"Lord Jesus," I cried, "help me!" as the car rolled three or four times and landed right side up in the middle of the road. I pulled the door latch and the door fell open, allowing me to climb out. I hear sirens approaching and notice that my arm is bleeding. A branch must have jabbed me through the open window as the car rolled, but the cut appeared to be minor.

The car, however, was in bad shape, smashed front to back and the top was caved in. All four tires had burst and the rims were bent. Emergency vehicles zoomed toward me from both directions, fire trucks, an ambulance, and the police. Someone at the airport must have spotted the crash and called for help.

The paramedic looked first at me, then at the car, and then back at me with an expression of disbelief.

"We need to get you to a hospital and have you checked out."

"No, I'll be ok," I assured him. "I just need to get home because I wasn't feeling well to begin with. He kept looking from me to the wrecked car, unable to fathom that I wasn't seriously injured. Eventually, they had me sign a form stating that I declined to be transported to the hospital and the ambulance left. A polite, soft-spoken police officer took my statement and offered me a lift to my apartment.

Some time later, my brother Kenny came bursting through the door, looking for me. The look on his face said it all. He had seen my car being carried on a flatbed and he was terrified that I might have been in a bad way. Sure enough, later that evening, the guys had to take me to the emergency room. The episode lasted a couple of days, and by the weekend I got my brother Moon to come up with his tools to see what we could scavenge from the Mustang, which was now sitting in a junkyard. I made a deal with the owner that if he let me grab a couple of items, he could have the vehicle to do as he pleased with, and he agreed.

Moon stared at the car, astonished that I hadn't been injured during the accident. While he pulled the engine, I opened the door to grab my stereo and some papers from the inside, and took a good look inside. The car was smashed on all sides, and the roof was caved in so badly in the back and on the passenger side that if anyone had been with me, they might well not have survived. The driver's seat, however, appeared to be in near perfect condition, as if there had existed some sort of cage, keeping me safe. I imagined the hand of God and recalled the prayer I'd uttered to Jesus as the car rolled over and over. Once again, Jesus had answered my cry.

We finished up and, as we were leaving, I took a final walk around the car and noticed that the sole thing on the exterior not damaged was the gas cap. I unscrewed the cap to take it with me, but it was attached to the car by a retaining screw. I grabbed a screwdriver from my brother and removed it. I still have it to this day, and installed it on what is now my third Mustang. That and the one before it have never been wrecked and I've raced them repeatedly. I feel that having that gas cap attached makes them blessed. I know that I am.

Katrina and I were talking more and more frequently now, and once in a while she and her cousin Melvina would show up on their bikes and hang out with us, laughing and joking around. At one time her mom, Ms. Nita I called her, showed up and marched them back home. She was letting us know that she didn't approve, but she was very gentle and very polite. I came to know and love her as a very sharp-minded, beautiful, and classy lady. Katrina continued to keep in touch and we talked about her life and her romancing and what it would be like if we got together.

"One day I'm going to just show up at your door and say go for it," she would tell me, "and you will know what that means." Sure enough, following her sixteenth birthday, Katrina showed up, alone, at my door. She smiled, looked me straight in the eye, and said, "Go for it!" From that moment she went from being a friend to the love of my life. I knew that I was too old for her, being twenty-one, but I was genuinely in love. The guys would often tease me about not being interested in "bird watching" anymore, after she and I became a couple. I only had eyes for her, and I wanted to do anything I could to make her happy. We were best friends and so much more. We went everywhere and did everything together.

I was looking at a *Pennysaver* magazine one day and spotted a listing for a $500 Mustang. I just couldn't resist, and scheduled an appointment to go and see it. The car was clean inside but it was a little beat up on the outside, an ugly green with a gold vinyl top and black repair patches on the rear fenders. The one thing that tempted me was that it was a rare model, a short-body 1972 Cobra edition with a 351 Cobra Jet engine. I handed over the money there and then, and the guy offered to let me take the car with his tags if I promised to return them the next day.

The car was really exciting to drive. It had no tail pipes, so it was a little loud, but I could feel the raw power it was ready to unleash anytime I put the slightest pressure on the accelerator. I couldn't wait to get it in the hands of my expert body man. Indeed, Karol was himself excited by the prospect of giving it a paint job.

As luck would have it, just as he was finishing up the paint job, I wrecked my beloved Oldsmobile. I'd been heading home on a Saturday afternoon and Kenny was just finishing up his training in the State Police Academy so he decided to roll with me. He fell asleep fairly quickly, and so I was just cruising along to my music. Just outside of Vienna I dozed off at the wheel. I awoke with a start to see a stoplight up ahead and a line of cars in front of me. I jammed on the brakes, but it was too late. I smashed into the car in front of me just as the light turned green and everyone began moving through the intersection. Kenny wasn't wearing a seatbelt, because they weren't required at that time, and he hit his head on the windshield, which cracked badly, giving him a small cut on his

Chapter Thirteen

forehead. The front end had taken a severe beating as well, and we had to call for my brother to bring a trailer to haul the car home. It never saw the road again.

I called Karol, who said the Mustang was ready, so I dropped in on him immediately. I was ecstatic with the job he had done. I had asked him to paint it a beautiful midnight blue and he had even re-dyed the top to make it a cleaner, brighter gold. He put gold pinstripes down it and made special outlines on the ram air hood. It was a really stunning job and I was just so proud to have it as my new hot ride. The car was just a dream to drive on the trips back and forth to the Shore. It was a total head turner and people commented about how sharp it was, everywhere I went. It was beautiful and it was strong. I got more kicks out of just cruising around and keeping it squeaky clean than I got out of racing it.

In 1984 I rode by this dealership and spotted a beautiful silver, red, and black Oldsmobile Cutlass. It was a special edition called the Hurst/Olds and I fell totally head over heels in love. It struck me as overpriced—$16,000 was way too much for an automobile back then and my salary or "lack thereof" was really going to make it a challenge to afford, but I had to have it. I drove home with my first-ever brand-new vehicle. Now, Katrina and I were riding in style.

The car was a real head turner and I became a police magnet. Most of them just wanted to check out the car, but some made up infractions to justify writing me a ticket. Some gave me great compliments while others seemed to be resentful, jealous even. There was one instance where I was almost shot by a police officer who was running radar right down the road from Goddard Space Flight Center. I decided to go on a lunch run to Laurel and took the back road called Soil Conservation Rd. Sure enough, just barely a half mile from base I come upon three Federal Park Police running radar and here one was flagging me down. He told me I was doing 43mph in a 35mph zone and he needed to see my license and registration. I reached into the glove compartment and pulled out the registration but when I reached for my back pocket for my wallet, which held my license, I saw the officer pulling his gun as if in a panic. As he raised the gun toward me I put my hands in the air and screamed "Wait! Wait!" and he kind of froze as if time had suddenly come to a halt. With his weapon still trained on me he said, "I asked you for your license and registration! I didn't ask you to go scratching around!" I said, "Officer if you're worried that I'm some kind of threat to you would you please call your partners standing there over here because I don't want to get shot. My license is in my wallet in my hip pocket and I'm not budging until you tell me to get it." Then he lowered the gun and told me to get the license. He wrote me a ticket for eight miles over the speed limit and told me I could go. I was so upset that all I could do was turn around and go back to the base. The anger in the guy's face stays with me to this day. I have to give God the glory for another miracle. I could have so easily become just another unarmed black man dead for "driving while black". What a chilling revelation.

Even at work I received mixed reactions to my having a brand-new vehicle instead of the older secondhand models I'd had up until then. One of my managers, Joe, offered me a promotion and sent me to HR to fill out the necessary paperwork. While I was there, the HR manager noticed an anomaly. The salary that Joe specified I be given, she said was twenty-five cents an hour less than the minimum posted for the job. She told me to let him know this and to give her a call if he wanted to correct it, and so I did.

"I thought I was doing you a favor as it was," he said, frowning.

I was taken aback. So, it wasn't just the Eastern Shore of Maryland that was full of racists. They were everywhere, and even those who smile at you to your face don't necessarily feel kindly toward you.

I had been working there for over five years and never received anything but "Exceeds expectations" on my reviews. Now this manager was looking me in the eye and telling me he was doing me a favor by increasing my responsibility while underpaying me. My idea of this being a great job had now shattered, and it didn't get any better while he was in our control center. One of the Mission Planners moved on to another job, and since the guys had already trained me on the duties, I filled in for him. I successfully juggled both jobs for a year, but when they decided to fill the position permanently, Joe told me he couldn't give it to me because it required a college degree. The fact of the matter was that they had targeted the position for one of the main office manager's sons. He came in, stayed about five or six months, and then moved on to something else.

I didn't bother to apply for the job this time and wasn't terribly surprised when they brought in a young white female with no experience. And, guess what? No degree either. I never said a word in protest, and I continued to do my work at "top notch level." Before the year was out, Joe was gone from the project. God, I suspected, had moved him from my path. The next manager was as different from Joe as night and day. Richard, or Dick, as he preferred to be called, was a very intelligent and compassionate guy who chafed at holding experienced people back simply because they did not have a degree. He didn't have a degree himself, but knew as much about the project and the instruments as likely anyone with a doctorate.

He seemed to take a special interest in me, would ask me questions about my illness, and began funneling me information and documentation on sickle cell disease. He introduced me to tapioca pudding and told me how it, along with yams, was the staple diet of the African people. I already knew that Africans had developed the sickle cell gene over a long period of growing immunity to malaria, and he and I had many conversations about it over the next few years. During this time, he always gave me fair salary increases. In one instance, the corporate office called to inquire about my long absences, seemingly evaluating whether they should keep me on. Dick quickly came to my defense, telling them that my being born with an illness was no fault of mine, and that I was the hardest-working employee he had. They considered it and, several days later, called him to say there was "no intent to chastise" me for it. I will never forget him going to bat for me in that way. He is still a great man in my eyes and, after thirty years, I still hear from him occasionally.

I was getting challenged to races more and more on the street, so I did some extra tuning and adding new performance parts to the Mustang. After quite a few runs, I managed to break the rear differential. I went to the salvage yard in Laurel and found another nine-inch rear. As I was leaving, one of the employees approached me to ask if I might be interested in a good motor. He said he had a car there of his own that he was giving up but it had a perfect 429-cubic-inch engine. I was skeptical, but he walked me over to

Chapter Thirteen

an old Ford LTD and, sure enough, he raised the hood and it was for real. Then he walked around to the driver's side door, reached in, and turned the key in the ignition. She fired up immediately and sat there, purring like a kitten. I couldn't believe it, but I confessed I only had a hundred dollars left after buying the rear. To my surprise he said, "I'll take it."

In less than twenty-five minutes he had cut the engine loose and lifted it onto the back of my brother's truck with a forklift. The next few weekends I would run home to help Moon get the Mustang back online. He engineered fitting the big block into the short body by creating his own motor mounts and cutting the fan shroud. When we'd finally finished, Moon shifted his attention to another task while I climbed in for a test drive.

Easing on down the road, I was struck by the different feeling this motor provided, in contrast to the smaller 351. The rear that I'd got from the junkyard had been fitted with a much stiffer gear ratio of 3:90 so the speedometer needed recalibration. When I reached the end of our road, at the American Legion, the moment of truth had arrived. I rolled out onto the straightaway and gunned it. Immediately it just smoked the tires and never stopped through first and second gear. I pushed to high gear early to get out of the burn and that worked. Now she was just climbing through the gear and the speedometer was buried in just over an eighth of a mile run. Before I reached the quarter mile, the tachometer was red-lining so I was forced to let up.

I was shocked and amazed, but knew I was a long way from street racing. There are not many ways to compete when you're spinning through two gears. The competition would be at the end of the run while I was still spinning tires.

I pulled over and raised the hood to make sure there were no leaks or anything to be concerned with. A Chevy Vega built for serious business pulled up, having been down the other end of the street when I'd lit up the road, and the driver wanted to race. I explained I couldn't, because I wasn't getting any traction. They had seen my maiden run so they couldn't argue the point and rolled on out looking for another chump to tangle with.

I returned to the house and explained everything to my brother. He tried it for himself and agreed that we had a bit more work to do. All the potential was there. We just had to figure out how to get it through the quarter.

To offset the low gear ratio, we put a taller tire on back. It still would fry the tires if I wasn't careful but now at least I had a chance to get off the starting line.

The first one to challenge the Mustang was my old roommate, friend and cousin. Josh was sporting a big-block Chevelle and was now considered the "top dog." Word traveled fast whenever there was a hot race about to go down. The Mustang's power was becoming known, but had not been tried yet. Most of the area didn't respect a Ford as having any potential at all—this was definitely Chevy country. Before we knew it people were showing up at the American Legion fast. That's where our races were usually staged. We would go down into the wooded area and race back to where my home street joined the main highway. We got lined up and I thought that I might have a chance, since he was running a four-speed manual shift, figuring he might also have a spinning problem. Sure enough, when the count of three came down and we cut loose, he did some twisting and burning off the line and so we came out pretty close to each other. As usual, the

Chapter Thirteen

Mustang did a heavy burn through first gear, but I got good traction when I pushed to second. When I pushed to third gear, the car surged. Josh had been holding about a car length ahead of me up until then, but when we blew through the finish line, we were side by side.

Everyone was arguing about who they thought had won. I conceded that he may have edged me by inches. Since he realized that he was being run down at the line, he wasn't too anxious to try again, but we did anyway. This time I came off the starting line right beside him and at that moment I knew I had him.

We came flashing through the quarter, with me leading by about a car length. The Mustang was now considered the "top dog." I drove back to the western side feeling pretty good that night.

The next weekend I came home as the one to beat and Josh was waiting. Rumors were flowing that he had done something new this week to get ready for the old Mustang. When we squared off, both cars had their share of burn off the line and we came out together. This was my clue that I would have the upper hand on the top end. Then something strange happened. When we went to high gear, the Chevelle made a sudden leap and began to pull away. He beat me by about two car lengths. Oddly enough, he didn't want to take time to talk about it either.

My brother Moon always rode with me now and sometimes he was the wheel man. As we headed home, he informed me that what we had just witnessed was the work of nitrous oxide. So now, as in a game of chess, it was my move. I was hooked on the feeling I'd got from the G-force pinning me back against the seat and the roar from a finely tuned big block. All week I thought about what to do next to get ahead of Josh. The answer was obvious. There is power in the "bottle." I couldn't build the motor too hot and continue to drive it a hundred miles each way every weekend—it just wouldn't hold up. With the 429 being totally stock right then, it was also totally dependable, so I decided to go for the new horsepower-in-a-bottle trick. I went to the speed shop on Friday and grabbed a 125-horsepower Power Shot from NOS.

As usual, most of us packed up and headed home, to the Shore. I didn't tell anyone about my little package, but I spent all day Saturday trying to install the new system. I knew that if no one spotted me, they would come looking for me on Sunday.

I managed to get the system installed and test it late that evening and, sure enough, the guys started showing up early Sunday afternoon. They were just itching to see a race but they were also trying to find out what I might have done to improve the Mustang's performance. Fortunately, Moon and I had already strategized and we were way ahead of them. We gave them nothing in response to their questions, and when they asked to see under the hood, we told them we had to chain it down because my hood latch was damaged. When they got down and looked, they could see the chain and padlock. At this point they were suspicious, but they didn't know enough to accuse us of being liars.

The yard filled up with cars and people. The trash talk was flying and we figured if we didn't cool them down, Mom and Dad would figure out what was up. We told them to go on down to our spot and we'd meet them there. We hung back a few minutes after they cleared out, trying not to look too obvious. When we climbed into the car to head out, there were Mom and Dad, in the doorway.

"Where are y'all going?" they inquired.

"Just running to the store," we said, but they weren't buying it.

"Y'all know better," Mom warned.

We pulled out of the yard very casually, heading in the direction of town. When we reached the Legion, it looked more like a block party. People were everywhere, making side bets on who would win. I felt kind of special when I looked around, and then I spotted my cousin Manney. Normally he never hung out to be a party to our mess, but he was the only true Ford lover I knew, other than my dad and brothers.

He smiled. "Are you going to take him?"

I grinned. "Oh yeah."

Moon and I cruise down to the starting line. Josh doesn't seem quite as confident or as cocky as he usually is, which strikes me as odd.

We square off and the three-count begins. His transmission is a four-speed manual shift and as we launch forward, we both go into a lot of tire burn. This plays to my advantage because he doesn't get much distance between us through the first gear. We grab second gear pretty much at the same time and the traction has now taken hold. He goes to third and starts to pull away, but I push to high gear and Moon ignites the nitrous from a switch on the dashboard. The Mustang surges forward and now I'm pulling away from him. Gator falls back and I shoot through the finish line alone.

"The shifter knob came off when I tried to get into fourth gear," he said, shrugging. "You up for another shot?"

This time he misses second gear and the race is over before it really gets started. I sail across the finish line, solo, and the crowd jeers, disappointed.

Manney, meanwhile, was smiling from ear to ear. It was his first time witnessing my Mustang's power and he was ecstatic. Although their top man was dethroned, the crowd had to give credit to the Ford and admit it was serious business. I went back to Mom and Dad's, had dinner, and then hit the road for home.

Yes, it was a good weekend and there would be many more ahead. The list of challengers began to grow and every weekend brought increased competition. One of our friends, Gary, had a '69 Chevelle and it was gorgeous. He had been racing long before I came on the scene and often competed against Josh and my brothers. He had been working on a new engine for a while and wanted to test how strong it was. The fact that I was running NOS was now old news to just about everyone.

We were hanging out at the club one night when he came up to me.

"Let me throw these five hundred horses at you and see what happens."

"Oh yeah," I said. "Let's go."

We cruised off to our favorite spot, thinking no one had noticed, but by the time we got lined up, there were cars and people gathering at the finish line, a reminder that nothing happened in that little town without someone noticing.

The count comes down and we're off.

Gary's car leaped ahead while I was still burning, twisting, and turning. To kill the spinning, I went to second gear early. The Mustang's rpm's dropped precipitously as a result, so I reached up and ignited the nitrous. To my surprise, the car snapped me back like I was tied to a rocket. Before I could even shift into third gear, I blew past Gary like he was standing still.

Chapter Thirteen

Midway through third, I knew the race was over and reached up to turn off the juice. As I approached the turnoff, which marks the finish line, the crowd was trying to prevent a car from pulling out of my parents' street and onto the main highway, but they refused to wait and pulled out directly into our path. I stomped on the brakes but all Gary saw was his chance to close the gap. Thinking he now had an opportunity to beat me, he came flying up beside me, only seeing the other car emerge and enter his lane. With me alongside, there was no way for him to avoid hitting one of us. Instinctively, I locked down hard on the brakes, giving him just enough space to whip into my lane and skirt the car in front of him. It was an incredibly narrow miss and I'm sure the woman driving the other car must have been shaken.

Back at the American Legion, Gary pulled up to where we stood, talking to the crowd, who were chattering madly and assuring us they had tried their best to stop the other car.

"Man, I'm never going to race you again," I told him. "That was a dangerous stunt you pulled."

"I know, man. That wasn't cool. Thanks for giving me a chance to get out."

We never raced again, but one weekend shortly after that, he came up to me inside the Legion and said some boys had come down from Salisbury and Cambridge and were harassing him to race. He wanted to know if I would have his back. I said ok and we walked outside. The lot was full of cars from all over, and the air was thick with arguments and boasts.

One of the guys from Cambridge shouted that he would give anybody there a three-car spot for $200. A hush blanketed the crowd.

"I'll take some of that action," I said.

One of the guys with them told his friend, "No, you don't want to do that." It was Braxton. Moon was dating his sister and they'd had a son together, so he knew me, or knew of me at least. Moon was nowhere to be seen, and I had no plans to actually race. But, despite the warning, the guy would not back down.

"What are you driving?"

I pointed to my stallion, sitting there, looking sleek and quiet. He immediately dismissed me for having a Ford and took the bet. We handed our money to one of the bystanders and off we went.

My brother Mike climbed in with me and we showed them where the starting line was.

"We're gonna take a quick ride further down, around the corner, just to make sure the cops aren't lying in wait," I said, and we headed off.

When we got around the corner, I jumped out, opened the trunk, and turned on the nitrous tank. Turning around, I headed back to the starting line. Someone counted the car lengths to afford us the promised three-count.

When the count came down, I nailed the gas. The Mustang was twisting and turning, but I could see in my rearview mirror that he was doing the same thing. I went to second and told Mike to flip the switch. When he did, it scared him because the force pinned him back against his seat.

Midway through third gear, my car popped and stumbled, but there was no way his Vega could make up the distance. We crossed the line with about the same three car lengths between us that we had begun with.

Chapter Thirteen

The crowd, having wanted to see the Ford go down, was subdued. Worried that I had hurt the engine, I pulled off the road, away from the crowd, and raised the hood to see what had gone wrong. The breather was still on, over the carburetor, and I had never turned the electric fuel pump on. In reality, we should have lost, because she was starving, trying to get through the quarter. I pulled off the air filter, turned on the fuel pump, and tested her on our return trip back to where the crowd was still gathered. To my relief, she was her old monstrous self again.

As I collected my winnings, Mike's brother-in-law Rocky came up to me.

"Man, the Mustang came through, but that Vega was sure sounding good."

I laughed.

"He can sound as good as he wants as long as he's behind me." I looked around. "We can go for another $200 with no spot."

The crowd went crazy, like wolves in a feeding frenzy. However, the driver of the Vega hesitated, because he knew now that he wasn't dealing with a slouch, and Braxton was still putting a warning word in his ear.

He challenged me instead to meet him at the racetrack the following weekend, where he could have his tires on for traction. I agreed, and Gary looked relieved, figuring the heat was off him. My bulging pockets felt good on the ride home.

The next weekend Mike and I went to the track to keep our date with the Vega. We put up another $200 and he told the tower to give me two tree lights ahead of him. I took off first, but the nitrous never ignited. The Vega caught up and passed me about midway down the track. Too late I realized I'd been running for weeks on the same tank and had forgotten to weigh the tank before I left. It was completely empty. All I could do was to congratulate him as he collected his winnings.

After that, I bought a spare tank to remedy the situation, intent on never being caught off guard like that again.

One other issue began to plague me after that, in the form of busted pistons. My old cast pistons were no longer holding up against the NOS and were crumbling, one by one. Each weekend, it seemed, one would chip or break up.

I would leave the car at Mom and Dad's and try to get back as early as possible the following Friday. Moon and I would grab a piston from an old junked motor, take the head off, and drop the base pan, remove the bad piston, install the spare, close her up, and test and tune her back to her old self. We had gotten so good at it that the guys were amazed by how they'd see the Mustang go home, broken, on Sunday only to see it right back out to play the next weekend. After about the fourth time though, I finally wised up and ordered a set of forged aluminum pistons. It was fortunate that, despite the crumbling pistons, the cylinder walls remained in very good condition. I never had to bore the engine and enjoy the idea of keeping the car as stock as possible. One nice bonus in changing to forged pistons was that I could now dial up from the Powershot 125 horsepower nitrous system. I got myself a Cheater 250 hp system, with three jet settings, but I never set it beyond the lowest setting, 175 hp. The Ford seemed to just love any little bit that I gave it, and the reaction was so powerful that it didn't require a lot.

Chapter Fourteen

Shortly after making these modifications, I went home one week to discover a new kid had arrived and was making waves as Princess Anne's next racing sensation. Dougie was a slim white guy and his family was rather well off. He had a '67 Camaro with a small block that was built from top to bottom. The car looked brand new, inside and out, and the suspension had been rebuilt to perfect specifications. It sported a 300 hp nitrous system and the folks were talking big-time smack. He hadn't targeted me yet, but he was devastating the locals, and so I knew it was just a matter of time before they pointed him in my direction.

Sure enough, one Sunday afternoon I was receiving calls at my parents' house from people asking me to come on down to the Legion. I ignored the calls until cars started showing up at the house. I couldn't tell if the locals were determined to see me upset today, or if they just wanted to see Dougie put in his place. Whatever the reason, they weren't willing to take no for an answer. Now, however, they were talking money, and that got my attention.

Moon and I made our little adjustments so the pony was breathing easy and running free before we eased on down the road. The Legion yard was packed and I was a little apprehensive, not by the prospect of taking on Dougie, but because some of the guys had already been out there lighting the road up and I wondered if the state police had caught wind of it. So, we waited a little while and then sent out guys in plain vehicles to check the roads on both ends. When they returned with an all-clear report, we dropped our hundred dollars in the hat and headed out. Wanting to add some weight in the back to improve traction, I asked our cousin Lionel to hop in. He was more than happy to oblige and off we went. Lionel, in top fighting form at the time, probably weighed at least 225 pounds.

We squared off at the line, the guys really rushing us about it. At the count of two Dougie prematurely blasted off. When I didn't move, he shut it down and backed up to the starting line.

Moon and I looked at each other in total disbelief. We had never seen anything take off that hard on the street in our lives. The car hadn't spun—it just raised up and launched, as if it had been shot out of a cannon. For the first time I felt apprehension at the prospect of a small-block Chevy. The count is to be on three, Dougie is reminded.

At the sound of three we both cut loose. Once again, the Camaro lurched ahead, like a ferocious beast, while we sat, twisting and sliding. By the time I got out of first gear, Dougie was already halfway through the quarter. I hit second gear and Moon hit the switch. Lionel spread his arms, gripping the panels on either side for stability as the Mustang screamed down the road, as if determined to catch the Chevy. As we roared toward him, it was as if Dougie had hit brakes. We blew past him, the Chevy rocking in our wake and looking like it was moving in slow motion as we zipped past at light speed. Lionel, still gripping the side panels, was grinning from ear to ear.

The guys at the finish line seemed mostly disappointed that a Ford had bested a Chevy again, but now some had become believers that a Ford could intercept a car that had initially been halfway through by the time the Ford got moving. There was no denying the top end power of the Mustang. She just never stopped pulling.

Dougie wasn't taking defeat lying down, however, and we raced many times after that, each time with the same results. He just couldn't hold us off through the full quarter mile.

Every week, after every race, he'd spend more money making changes to try and get ahead.

The final time we raced, I had been hanging out with Josh and one of his buddies on a Saturday night, who were testing and tuning their own cars to get ready for Dougie the next day. They must have raced each other back and forth half the night. When I showed up, they were preparing for their last trial run. We talked and joked awhile and then headed out. They didn't want to draw undue attention by going to our standard spot, so they headed out through Perry Hawkin, past where our grandma used to stay. They lined up on the straightaway, counted off, and cut loose. Oddly enough, they came through side by side, with Josh winning by a nose.

Josh still wasn't sure how to gauge his chances against Dougie the next day so he turned to me.

"Let's try it," he urged.

I figured he'd really have to smoke me, since I wasn't turning on the bottle—that would be the only way he'd have a chance with Dougie. So, we went down and squared off. As usual, my burning and twisting enabled him to get out in front, but I froze his progress when I went to second gear. When I shifted again, the Mustang started reeling him in. It pulled him back so strongly that I managed to catch him at the line. If I'd had another ten feet to go, I would have beaten him. He was happy, not knowing the true circumstance, but when he asked me to try his buddy, I said no, that I couldn't let them go out and make me the chump for the evening. If he wanted me to race his buddy, I would be forced to turn on the juice. He froze and looked at me in disbelief.

"You had it on," he insisted.

I shook my head.

"Show me," he demanded.

I opened the trunk and turned the valve to activate the flow of nitrous. He knew the truth as soon as he heard the pressure hiss as the gas rushed up the line, but he still wasn't wholly convinced.

"Let's try it again!" he urged me.

"No man, you don't want to do that."

"Then race my buddy," he insisted.

I tried to talk them out of it, but their minds were made up, convinced I was somehow trying to pull a fast one on them. So off we went to the starting line. As usual, he leaped out in front. Meanwhile, I'm still babying the pony out of the gate. But when I shifted into second gear, I ignited the juice and we flew toward him. By the time I pushed to high gear, we were past him, at which point I reached over to shut the bottle down. We were still carrying so much force that I hit the finish line about five car lengths ahead of him.

Chapter Fourteen

They gave up and headed home. I watched them go, thinking Dougie was going to eat them for breakfast.

The next morning my brother came in and woke me up. He wanted to know what had happened the night before, because the word all over town was that Josh had beaten me and was now calling Dougie out. I told him what had occurred and my belief that neither of them had any chance of beating Dougie.

Nonetheless, by noon everybody was worked up and cars started appearing in the yard. Apparently, this showdown was not going to be at the Legion. They wanted to go back in the country, where Josh and I had battled the night before.

Sure enough, after a while, we see both Josh and Dougie cruise by the house, heading out to the old back road. We jumped into our cars and headed out after them, joining the huge train of cars. When we reached the road where the action would take place, it was a carnival-like atmosphere. Cars and people were everywhere, men, women, and children.

I pulled Josh aside.

"Man, why did you tell everybody you beat me when you know what the deal was? I was just trying to help you out."

He shrugged and busied himself getting ready.

Last time I'd give anybody a free pass again, I thought.

I cruised on down to the starting area and pulled off onto a side road. Moon pulled up alongside and we sat and watched the preliminaries, all the smaller fish flexing their muscles.

One of the guys eventually challenged Moon's Javelin to a two-car spot, something he couldn't turn down.

Much like Dougie the first time we'd raced, the challenger jumped the two-spot mark and was beside the Javelin by the count of three. Moon deliberately sat there, not moving, until they flagged the guy down to come on back.

Moon told him to forget about the offered two-car spot and to line up side by side. This time the other car waited until the count of three. Moon and his Javelin wiped the street with him. It wasn't even close.

Moon and I had a laugh about how they had just tried unsuccessfully to play him.

When Josh was ready, he and Dougie came down and squared off at the line. At the count of three, I saw what I'd expected: It was all Dougie. He launched out in typical cannonball fashion. Josh never had a chance.

By this time, Dougie was feeling particularly cocky. He returned immediately to the starting line and pointed at me, tauntingly. I was more than happy to oblige by that point, so we cranked up and pulled out onto the street. I clearly wasn't thinking, because I knew perfectly well that racing my car in a cooled-down state would totally annihilate the tires.

We pulled straight up to the line beside Dougie and the count began. When he launched, my car did a twist and shout all over the road. By the time we got lined back up and broke the burn, Dougie was halfway to the finish line. I pushed to second, Moon lit up the juice, and the car screamed so hard down the road, it was trembling. I pushed to high gear as fast as I could and held on tight.

We blew by him right at the finish line, but he came so close to making it through that he declared victory and refused to pay.

I didn't say a word, but the guys who'd been watching told him he was mistaken and that, in essence, he was reneging on a bet, something you just didn't do.

He sent for me to come and retrieve the money, but I wasn't interested in talking to him at that point. Still, the guys insisted that we settle things, so I went over to him, he paid up, and we were done.

***

Throughout this period, I had Katrina by my side. She attended our group gatherings, parties, and picnics, and even my coworkers came to recognize her. She traveled down to the Shore with me almost every weekend.

By the time she went off to Salisbury State College, I began to notice changes in the way we treated each other. Even our greetings had shifted slightly. We had spent five years together and only in the last year did I come to realize that she needed to experience life outside of our relationship. She had grown to be a beautiful, strong, and independent young woman who was now ready to spread her wings and fly solo. It was difficult to accept, but I knew that I had to let her go or our relationship risked becoming the source of a lot of ugly, heartbreaking memories.

She went out and found a car that she liked, a Nissan 200SX, and I helped her fix and dress it up real nice. I got my cousin Karol to give it a nice paint job and, as always, he did an exceptional job. It was a deep burgundy with black and silver stripes. We topped it off with a set of fog lights that complemented the headlights and parking lights with a perfect v-line coming down to meet each other. It was a head turner, day or night, and you could spot it from anywhere. She loved it, and it gave her the ability and freedom to stretch out more on her own.

Chapter Fifteen

My buddy Larry and I had been hanging out a lot, playing basketball, volleyball, softball, and bowling. We were forever joining teams, although rarely did we play on the same team. I played mostly with the guys on the Nimbus Project and Larry often played with the Landsat or Multisat groups. After games we would get together and go someplace for a couple of beers and maybe something to eat.

After a while, we would have drinks for lunch. One day, we returned to work and I was drunk. That bothered me, but what was worse, I clearly wasn't very good at hiding it. Ed was casually chatting with me and I'm not sure if he smelled the alcohol or whether I was just acting goofy, but all of a sudden he asked, "Are you all right, Collins?"

I tried to play it off and assured him I was ok but for the rest of the day I hid out at my desk as much as possible. After that, I made a point of cutting back and sometimes I would make excuses to Larry and claim that I had something else to take care of at lunchtime.

Chapter Fifteen

I wonder whether the alcohol might have been a contributing factor to my escalating bouts with sickle cell. He and I still had some crazy times out in the streets together, however.

One night we got together with Rebecca and Benita, our co-workers and friends, and went bowling. Unfortunately, we ran into some locals who saw us only as two black guys getting way too cozy with two white ladies at the bowling lanes in Riverdale, joking and snacking as we knocked down ten pins. The nasty comments from nearby became audible and when we looked over, they were staring us down.

The girls were getting agitated and began to fling comments back at them.

"I think we'd better go," I murmured to Larry, and we convinced the girls to leave. But when we got outside, we found that all four tires on Rebecca's car had been slashed. It was ugly. Rebecca called a friend to rescue us, who gave us a ride back to our cars. From then on, we always made sure that if we went out with the girls, it would be in a group and not resemble two couples out together. I'm still friends with them to this day.

On New Year's Eve, I decided it would be best for Katrina if we made a clean break. My friend Vanessa had noticed that I was no longer exclusive with Katrina and decided to introduce me to her roommate, arranging for us to meet at Club Meade, the officers club at Fort Meade, for their New Year's party. My brother Mike was also having a party that night, so I went there first to let Katrina know that it was over.

After saying goodbye to her, I left for Fort Meade, where Vanessa had arranged for me to meet Shari Witherspoon. Shari turned out to be a beautiful, quiet soul with a kind and sensitive, yet fun-loving spirit. But the club was so packed, we were not able to get in. We tried a few other places but the result was the same—every place was packed.

"Let's just get ourselves a bottle of Champagne and go back to my house," she suggested.

At midnight, we toasted the New Year and then she sent me home. In the days that followed, I felt like a little lost puppy and began to look for reasons to contact Katrina, even though she welcomed the space between us now. I finally accepted that there was no turning back the clock when one day I found her hanging out with my cousin Mason and some friends. I asked her to sit in the car and talk to me for a moment. She hesitated but agreed. As we sat, chatting, I spotted a car behind me that was trying to get past, so I started the car and moved forward slightly to give them room to get by. Katrina sat upright and asked where I was going, the panic in her voice conveying her concern as to what I was up to. Did she think I'd been stalking her? That I would abduct her?

It broke my heart that she could possibly think that I would endanger her in any way. I apologized and explained, as the other car inched past us, evidence to support that what I was saying was true.

Not long afterward, I learned that she had grown interested in someone else. Early one Sunday morning I found myself ringing the doorbell of her home. I knew she wasn't there, but I explained to her mother, Ms. Nita, that I would not be coming around anymore.

"I'm getting ready to go to church," she said, and looked at me intently. "Why don't you come with me?"

I didn't really want to go, but I couldn't say no to her any more than I could say no to Katrina. We headed off to this little church on a hill, Queen's Chapel United Methodist Church. The music was good and everyone was very friendly. Then the pastor got up to speak his message. I sat, spellbound, listening to him. It was as if he were telling my life story, my life's experiences, from the pain of sickness to the failed relationships.

The next thing I knew, was I had made it down the aisle and was being embraced by Rev. Kess as he opened the doors to the church. Tears were flowing down my face, and I gave my life to Jesus right then and right there. Ms. Nita, it turned out, had saved my life.

I felt peace within for the first time that I could remember, and able to let go of Katrina and let her get on with her life. With each new week I grew stronger in the knowledge of my Lord.

Rev. Kess and I grew close over time and had many heart-to-heart talks.

"Don't put your trust in people," he would counsel, "but always trust in the Lord. People are only human and can fail you at any moment, but God's love never fails."

I found myself developing an insatiable yearning for God's Word, and read and meditated on the Bible every day. I found myself consciously making decisions with God's will in mind. Every day it was as if I were high on Jesus, and it was the best feeling in the world. I was allowing the Lord to guide my footsteps and He was showing me new things every day.

My attitude toward women became one of respect and appreciation. Although Shari showed little interest in a relationship with me, I turned my focus toward developing a courtship with her, coaxing her out to see a movie or let me take her out to dinner, so we could get to know each other better.

Vanessa encouraged Shari to give me a chance, but Shari was reluctant. Our friendly dates continued for about five months, with us just getting together once every week or two. She seemed content with that, but I was in no hurry to get into anything heavy. I had decided to put it all into God's hands, and prayed that I would not get involved with anyone until I was convinced that He had presented me with the right lady. That's when Vanessa stepped in again. She suggested I pick up another bottle of Champagne and drive Shari out to a spot Vanessa had told me about, a park-like setting with a river running through it along which beautiful boats cruised past. I didn't think too much of it at the time, but it sounded like a pleasant enough idea.

Shari and I sat on the hood of the car, drinking our Champagne and watching the boats float by. Our conversation was happy, light, and relaxed, just two friends enjoying spending time together and getting to know each other better.

It was a beautiful day. I didn't know how special it had been for Shari until Vanessa saw me the next day. She beamed as she shared how Shari told her just how much she had enjoyed our time together.

"I think you really won her over this time," Vanessa said, delighted.

Shari and I began to get together more frequently. She would sometimes stop by on her way to work. I would cook dinner and make her a plate to take to work for lunch. She seemed to really enjoy my cooking and I really enjoyed cooking for her.

Chapter Fifteen

My brother Darryl was the first one of my family to meet her, although it turned out not to be under the happiest of circumstances. We had bought some crabs and stopped by Darryl and Tracy's place to hang out. While eating the crabs, Shari suffered an allergic reaction which caused her upper lip to swell to about three times its normal size. Fortunately, that's as serious as it got, and Darryl, being the maniac that he is, started teasing her right off the bat. She recovered pretty quickly and we laughed it off.

He would often tease us that we were carrying on an undercover relationship, because we were so low-key around each other. When he played softball with my team at Goddard, he noted that Shari never paid me undue attention and that I never singled her out for attention either. She was a very private individual, and was determined not to let her coworkers know that we were an item yet. So he dubbed us the "Undercover Lovers".

When the Fourth of July rolled around, my sister Belinda organized a pool party. I invited Shari to accompany me. It would be the first time she would meet the entire family. I picked her up after work and we had a wonderful time. My family, always wild and crazy, teased and harassed her in an affectionate way that made her feel totally accepted.

Up until now we had not been physically intimate.

"Are you going to send me home alone again?" I asked, when I dropped her off by her car. I was only half-teasing but was startled when she replied, "No, you can come home with me." We had taken more than six months to get to know each other and I found myself totally devoted to her. I was operating on a whole different level, now that I felt I had God overseeing my steps.

Fewer weekends were spent back home as we began going to more and more places together, seeing so much that was new to me. We would go on shopping trips, or visit her extended family, which was spread around North Carolina, Virginia, in Norfolk and Virginia Beach, and Baltimore. We had a wonderful time our first Super Bowl weekend. It was a planned trip to Atlantic City with a bunch of our friends. Larry and Debra were right there hanging out with us the entire time. We were not too interested in the gambling scene so we spent most of our time hanging out on the boardwalk, playing games and walking the beach. We searched for good restaurants to eat and on Sunday many of us gathered in one hotel suite to watch the big game. We had a blast cheering and arguing about our favorite team. The bus ride home was a pure joy and closed out a highly memorable weekend. I was less focused on myself and allowing God to be my center.

After nearly two years of courting Shari, I had the opportunity to do something I had never done before. Vanessa, her family, and friends had organized a trip to Hawaii, and Shari, her mom, and her brother Jerry were geared up to go, and I was invited as well. I was now considered one of the gang, and Daniel, Sheila and Rose were all a part of the crew taking part in the trip. This would be my first time ever on an airplane. The doctors had warned that the pressurized cabin of an airplane could possibly send my system into crisis, so I was somewhat nervous, but once we boarded the plane and all of us were seated in a group, I forgot my fears and we laughed and clowned all the way there, stopping first at Ft. Worth, Texas, to change to a huge 747 for the last leg, over to Hawaii.

I looked around the immense plane, astonished that anything its size and weight could even get off the ground.

Chapter Fifteen

The journey took a total of eleven hours and we were glued to the windows as we approached the Islands, peering out and marveling at what was truly the most beautiful sight any of us had ever seen. The water was so clear and blue that you could see straight to the bottom in most places. The Islands looked like a page from a magazine or book. It was just awesome.

When we landed, natives stood outside the terminal, waiting to greet us with leis, and we could take pictures with them. The young lady I took a photo with was extremely tall and the guys chuckled to see her towering over my head. We all laughed to see Momma Doris standing there, smiling, with a young man who was taller than she was, yet probably younger than her children. Papa Spoon, on the other hand, is probably a foot shorter than she is and he always wants to duck from the camera when anyone wants to take a picture of the two of them.

We were in Hawaii. It felt like a dream.

We took a shuttle to the hotel, eagerly taking in all of the sights, buildings, and people along the way. The hotel was beautiful, elegant, everything we could have wanted. Shari, her brother Jerry, and I shared one room and snapped countless pictures of each other on the balcony that overlooked the city and the beach. As soon as we got our bags into our rooms, we headed out to tour the grounds, taking pictures of ourselves surrounded by beautiful trees, rocks, and sand. We took various tours around Oahu to visit the pineapple fields, historic palaces, and the famous statue of King Kamehameha.

Our first night, we went to a club inside the hotel. We ordered Mai Tais and piña coladas, and I was struck how fresh the fruit was that garnished our drinks. I'd never tasted strawberries or pineapple as delicious as those in my life. I actually enjoyed the fruit more than the drinks!

The next day, we visited Diamond Head Crater. The tour bus stopped en-route, along a little narrow road, and we were told we could select a mango from one of the trees or among those on the ground. I picked one up off the ground and it looked just perfect, not a single blemish or bruise, but I had no idea what a fresh mango was or what it was supposed to taste like.

Later, back at the hotel, I washed it, peeled back the skin, and sat out on the balcony to eat it. It absolutely blew my mind. I was instantly in love. The flavor exploded in my mouth. It was so juicy and sweet that the liquor ran down my arm when I bit into it. Unforgettable, sitting enjoying this fruit in its beautiful, native paradise. (I still love anything with mango in it, but, unfortunately, the mangoes imported to the U.S. mainland have never once compared with what I ate in Hawaii.

Chapter Sixteen

One of the next spots we visited was the Koolau Mountain Range. It was very high and we stopped at a beautiful lookout point. The cliffs were steep and the wind strong, making it rather scary when we ventured too close to the edge. The guide told us the legend of a young man who had lost his sweetheart to a tragic accident. He was so heartbroken that he decided to kill himself by jumping off the cliff, but every time he tried to jump, the wind caught him and carried him back to the cliff top. He finally gave up, taking it as a sign that his sweetheart wanted him to live.

Towards the end of the first week of our two-week trip, we visited the gorgeous Hanauma Bay. We took the long hike around the bay to an isolated spot, a famous natural pool known as the Toilet Bowl which features a huge hole in the lava rock. When waves flow into the cove, the hole fills up and then flushes the water out again, like a toilet.

Not being much of a swimmer, I was afraid of being sucked out to sea through the hole, so I stood on the edge and watched as everyone else hopped in and waded around.

When we returned to the main part of the bay, we were offered the opportunity to try snorkeling. The fish and the coral, we were told, was "a must see." I was determined to give it a try, despite not being a particularly good swimmer, because the water was very shallow—I don't think it ever got any higher than my chest. The staff at the rental place gave us a quick how-to instruction demo and off we went. We had a ball. Some of the guys had underwater cameras and got great shots of the coral and surrounding sea life. The fish were extraordinarily colorful and just as curious about us—and arguably more fearless—as we were about them. They would swim right up to us, ducking or dodging when we tentatively reached out to touch them.

However, all of that climbing around the rocks and pumping my legs through the water with the flippers on my feet took a toll on me. By the time I had returned my snorkeling equipment, I felt a familiar dull throbbing in my knees.

I decided I would lie out on the sand and let the sun bake into my bones, hoping that would ease the pain, until everyone was done, but by the time we were ready to go, my legs were aching badly. When we got back to the hotel, I knew I was in serious trouble. I skipped dinner that night, eager to rest enough to get back on my feet. Shari got me Tylenol for the pain and I tried to sleep it off, but eventually the pain escalated to where I found it almost unbearable to just walk to the bathroom and back during the night. I had one more week left to spend on this idyllic island and all I could think about was how would I manage to fly back home if I couldn't get my legs in shape in time.

The next day, everyone came by to check on me. I assured them that I would be all right with some rest, but the discussion turned to locating an urgent care facility. Rose decided she would nurse me back to health and bring me food and drink. The no-sodium

Soup she returned with was the most awful-tasting stuff I'd ever eaten (something we still laugh and joke about to this day).

"Are you trying to heal me or kill me?" I demanded, and everyone laughed. On day two of my being in bed, Vanessa, Shari, and Rose took me to the closest hospital. The doctors there hadn't a clue how to treat sickle cell, but they managed to get enough information to put me on oxygen and an IV drip, where I remained for a few hours before they then released me with a short-term prescription for pain. They told me to come back for an examination to ensure it was safe for me to fly home.

Now the worry was what to do if I couldn't fly home. My best childhood buddy, Tammy, was stationed in Hawaii with the military, so I called and left a message explaining that I might need her help for a day or two, if I couldn't leave with everyone else. I had no idea what her living situation was, or even if civilians were allowed to stay on the base.

Meanwhile, I had three full days to get myself well enough to travel; the fourth was the day of our flight. Everyone brought food and drink to keep my strength up. Ms. Shirley, Mom Doris, and all of the older ladies traveling with us prayed together to ask God for His healing mercy.

Two days before we were due to fly out, I had begun to feel a bit better, so much so that I managed to accompany everyone on our last scheduled tour, a boat ride around the island, which didn't sound like it'd be too taxing.

Onboard, there was music, dancing, and drinks were served continually. As the cruise neared the end, the crew, who had demonstrated some dances for us, began to pull people up onto the dance floor to try their hand at some. A couple of them zoomed in on me and tried to physically drag me to the floor. Everyone in my group was arguing that I couldn't do it, to stop trying to get me to dance, but they wouldn't listen until Jerry jumped up and started dancing for me. I don't think they realized until later, when I needed help getting off the boat. But despite my limitations, It was a fun time and I'm glad I was able to make the most of one of our last days there.

My last day in Honolulu was very low key. I managed to join everyone for lunch and dinner and drank only water, copious amounts of it, throughout the day to hydrate as best I could and just slept and watched TV in my room the rest of the time, retiring early before I had to return to the hospital ahead of the flight in order to get their ok to travel. They checked my blood gases, decided that I was sufficiently recovered, and cleared me to travel.

We hurried back to the hotel, grabbed our bags, and joined the line for the shuttle to the airport. Hours later, the plane lifted off on time, and I'm happy to say I was on it and feeling grateful that God had answered all of our prayers and appreciative of His goodness and mercy. His presence in my life continued to be evident, wherever I went.

Chapter Seventeen

Wanting to push my fitness level up a notch, I joined another karate club. The Taekwondo club in Laurel was starting a new class, and after an initial interview with the Sensei, I agreed to start training. It was very grueling but definitely a lot of fun.

Because of my previous training in Kenpo, I excelled very quickly in this new art. It was arguably a bit unfair to have me spar with less experienced students who had started training in the new class when I did, so after a while, I found myself sparring with the older, more advanced classes with students who were at higher levels of skill. I managed to hold my own and moved up the chain pretty quickly. Before too long, I was helping to train students who had started at the same time I had, as fellow beginners. It was a great experience.

After three years of courtship, Shari and I had begun to talk about the future. She was making it clear that she was in it for the long haul. When I would get sick, I'd warn her about what the future held, and tell her she didn't need to feel she was stuck with me. She refused to be swayed.

"You're not getting rid of me," she'd retort, looking me straight in the eye.

We talked about having children and my fear of bringing kids into the world who might inherit my disease. I didn't want to see our children suffer.

Shari went to the doctor and got tested for the sickle cell trait. It came back negative. She was trying to assure me that we would be ok, but I didn't want her to have to watch me die either. The frequency of my episodes was increasing, and it depressed me.

By now, almost all of my brothers and cousins had moved on to the next phase of their lives. Baby Tommy had moved up to this side of the shore to work at the prison in Jessup, as a guard. He and I rented an apartment together for about a year. After that, the new prison on the Eastern Shore opened and he put in for a transfer.

When he left to return home, Darryl and I became roommates. His was the only name on the lease, but we split the rent equally and the two of us got along pretty well together for the first few months.

I had been out with Shari and some friends one night, and it was pretty late when I came in. I entered the apartment, locked the door, and started for my bedroom. I jumped when Darryl, always a bit high-strung, charged out of his room, brandishing his police weapon and raising the gun in my direction.

"Hey!" I shouted, alarmed. "It's me! What are you doing?"

When he realized who I was, he relaxed, but I was furious. No way was I going to go through that again! How could it not have occurred to him that it might be me, his roommate?

I have never liked guns. I began alerting him whenever I came in late, before I closed the door. And I began looking for other living arrangements.

Chapter Seventeen

In December 1987, I started contemplating what to give Shari for Christmas. Thinking back at the three years we'd been together, it dawned on me that we had never once exchanged an angry word with each other. We didn't necessarily agree on everything all of the time, but when we did differ, we talked about it and never raised our voices to each other.

Maybe God had, in fact, already answered my prayer that I didn't get involved with anyone except the one He wanted me to be with, someone, I'd specifically said, who would love me as much as I loved them. It was time to get serious about life and make the most of the time that God was giving to me.

I called my buddy Larry and asked him to come with me to shop for a ring. I think he was even more excited than I was. He was bubbling over with encouragement and praise.

He was also enjoying a new relationship with the love of his life, and had moved on to another project, to LANDSAT, another earth observatory satellite. It was there that he met Debra and they couldn't be happier. They also were, he confessed, contemplating tying the knot.

We went to the mall, and into Kay Jewelers. One ring caught my eye, one which personified our love, I felt. It wasn't too big or too small, and was quite different from the rest, with a larger center diamond flanked by three smaller diamonds on either side. The salesperson said it was unusual because it was a new design. It was a little steep price-wise, but my heart was set on it.

I applied for store credit and the next I knew, we'd completed the sale. I just needed sufficient time to pay it off.

I had decided by that time that I didn't want to give Shari an engagement ring for Christmas, as that would mean it was a

Christmas present—I wanted it to mean more, much more. So, I bought her several Christmas gifts and kept the ring hidden, despite her dropping several hints about a certain gift for her finger. I stuck to my guns, determined not to link such an important occasion to Christmas.

When Christmas Day rolled in we got together and had a ball. I had the feeling she was expecting more, but she never once indicated that she was disappointed in any way.

I had chosen what I thought would be the perfect day to propose—New Year's Eve, the anniversary of our first date as arranged by Vanessa.

New Year's Eve! That had to have been the longest week in history, between Christmas Day and year end, as I waited impatiently to pop the question. There were no family parties planned or talk of anything special going on. In fact, Shari was scheduled to work the midnight shift so we decided to celebrate with dinner and a Champagne toast before she had to leave for work.

I cooked dinner and we sat, ate, and reminisced about past New Year's events, this being our fourth anniversary, and how we might celebrate when her break came around.

Without warning, I stood and then got down on one knee. Would you marry me, I asked?

Her eyes filled with tears.

"Yes!"

Celebrating our fourth anniversary became our commitment to a life together, forever.

She called a few family and friends to excitedly share the good news and everyone shared that excitement. She didn't want to go to work, but reliability and her word are a huge part of who she is.

Chapter Seventeen

Reluctantly, we kissed goodnight and she drove off. She called me, as always, to let me know she had arrived safely, but this time we talked a little longer, her excitement still evident.

The days that followed were busy with all sorts of decisions that had to be made. I still faced the task of talking to Papa Spoon about asking for his daughter's hand. He was a tough customer when it came to his one and only daughter. He called her his Sugar and no one could mess with her and get away with it. Fortunately, I had been coming around for nearly four years now, and he had warmed to me.

When I sat down to talk to him, he was very quiet and I was very nervous. Everyone had warned me that if I ever wanted to marry Shari, I had to get past both Mr. Walter, Vanessa's dad, and Papa Spoon, who were both inordinately protective of her.

"Would you give me your blessing to marry your daughter?"

I felt a flicker of nervousness when he didn't look at me directly. He lowered his head slightly.

"What did Sugar say?"

"She said yes."

He nodded almost imperceptibly. I swallowed, the sound incredibly loud to my ears in the silence.

He got to his feet and looked directly at me.

"That's my Sugar," he said, possessively.

"Yes sir, I know."

He walked out without another word. I had been put on notice that I had better treat her right. That part I wasn't worried about. That was just what I intended to do.

We decided not to rush into it and, instead, focus on sorting through what clutter there was in our lives. I had debt to dispense with, and medical bills still hovering over me.

We chose the spring of the following year, 1989, to hold our ceremony. Vanessa was planning her wedding to Ron that coming fall, and as the time drew closer, she elected to move in with Ron ahead of the wedding, but she was reluctant to leave Shari to live by herself in the house Vanessa had bought in Baltimore County. She asked if we were interested in staying in the house together, and maybe purchase it from her later, as a starter home.

We had been spending so much time with my family lately that it seemed like a good idea to enable her to stay where she was, closer to her family. Vanessa gave us a break on the rent and, during the summer of 1988, I moved to Baltimore and Shari and I continued making plans for our spring wedding. I was relieved not to have to look for an apartment to rent and felt I was off to a solid start on my new life.

There was just one problem. When I got sick, it proved hugely inconvenient to have Shari take me all the way to Howard University Hospital, in Washington, D.C. I also didn't want her traveling back and forth through D.C. to visit me when I was in the hospital. So, the first time I got sick in Baltimore, I gave St. Agnes Hospital, fairly close to home, a try. It turned out to be a very unpleasant experience.

When I arrived at the emergency room, doubled over in pain, they put me in the back, on a gurney behind a little curtain, and wouldn't permit Shari to accompany me. By this time I was rolling from side to side, I was in so much pain. After what felt like an eternity, a doctor appeared by the curtain and, without approaching any closer, demanded to know in a very loud voice what the problem was, what drugs had I taken, and were they illegal drugs—was I a junkie? I could hardly talk because I was short of breath and my chest was throbbing, but between gasps I explained that I was in the midst of a sickle cell crisis and needed treatment for the excruciating pain. He looked at me, suspiciously, indifferent to my distress, and continued to jab me with questions, despite my inability to speak without great effort. The sound of his voice was hitting me like someone was plunging knives into my chest and I couldn't stand it another second.

"Just leave me the hell alone!" I gasped in frustration. "If you can't help me, then just get away from me!"

He left me writhing in pain. Eventually, convinced they weren't going to help me, I managed to muscle myself out of bed, grabbing anything and everything to hold myself upright as I made my way toward the entrance, looking around desperately for Shari.

A nurse spotted me and came to my assistance.

"Where are you going?" she asked.

"Anywhere," I gasped, unable to stand up straight with the pain. "It's clear nobody's going to help here."

"Come back to bed and lie down," she coaxed, and guided me back to bed. "I'll find the doctor."

"Please," I begged, "not the doctor I just saw. Please, not him! Call Howard University Hospital, and ask for Dr. Castro. He can tell you about me and what to do. I need something for this pain," I gasped.

She left and returned with the second of the only two doctors on ER duty that night. He had heard of Dr. Castro and knew something about his work. He ordered some meds and stayed with me until the IV bag arrived, inserted it himself, gave me oxygen, and administered the first dose of pain medicine. I could have kissed him.

After a few hours, they decided to admit me, and Shari had been allowed in to be with me. They moved me upstairs. I was heavily medicated so I slept most of the time I was there. Without fail, every time I awoke, Shari was sitting right there, next to the bed, staring right at me with concern.

I lost track of time. Whenever someone arrived for my next shot of pain medication, I begged her to go home and get some rest that she didn't need to sit there and watch me sleep. Most of the time she just stayed, but on a few occasions, she would go home, unquestionably exhausted.

Then something odd happened. I was lying there, eyes closed, half awake, when I heard a voice clearly say, "I love you, and I'll never leave you."

I opened my eyes looked around, expecting to see Shari, but she wasn't there. I was alone. I stayed in the hospital for about two weeks and was so glad when I got to the point where I didn't need the injections anymore. I always had this fear that I might get hooked on pain medication, and there were times I would lie there and try to tough it out and not ask for the shot, until I just couldn't take it anymore. Sometimes I would lie there and quietly cry.

Chapter Eighteen

Getting released from the hospital, as always, felt like I'd been given a new lease on life. I walked into the house and feel a sense of peace wash over me as I drank in the calm and familiarity of our home.

"Thank you, Jesus," I murmured.

After a few days of being home and moving around, I was ready to go back to work. Invariably, after every absence, the guys always greeted me with great affection I'd been on the job by then for nine years and, sadly, the Nimbus Project was starting to wind down. The young lady, Samantha, who had come in completely inexperienced and been given the job of mission planner instead of me, had become a good friend. I never minded that it had propelled her on the path to promotions that I would never see. She became an online evaluator while I remained a data technician, but I was grateful to have sustained my position despite all of my bouts of sickness, whereas my brother David struggled to remain employed and, at one point, had been declared disabled. Perhaps my illness played a role in my not getting promoted, as I did miss a lot of time.

Still, Sam and I got along great. We went to lunch together, and sometimes we would pick up lunch for everyone in the control center, before we eventually decided to pool our money and buy meat, bread, and condiments to make lunch for several days. One day, while making our lunch, Bob came over and jokingly demanded to know why he hadn't been invited to join us, ribbing us to no end about how selfish we were and how he didn't like the new cliques we were forming. Abruptly, to our astonishment, he belted out a quick ditty, opera-style.

> *The lunch bunch, the lunch bunch,*
> *Ricky, Perry, and Sam.*
> *The lunch bunch, the lunch bunch,*
> *Roast beef, salami, and ham!*

He'd even gotten the menu right.

We had such great times back then, but times were changing rapidly, as the company focused on how to whittle and ultimately phase out the project.

Vanessa and Ron tied the knot as planned, in the fall, and Larry and Debra held their wedding ceremony about a week later. Shari and I were both in Vanessa's wedding party and I was Larry's best man. Both ceremonies were awesome, and yet different as night and day. Vanessa and Ron were married in a beautiful mansion while Larry and Debra were married in the beautiful garden that was Debra's brother's backyard. It was a happy time.

Meanwhile, at work, a couple of our programmers devised writing a program that would automate the data processing section of the project, which would make the Bendix crew on the other side redundant, which naturally upset them. I assisted our programmers with the data entry and computer testing, not realizing at the time that my position would also be eliminated, were it successful.

In January, Dick called me in to inform me that my position was being eradicated, but that he had been looking for opportunities for me with other projects and had found an opening for a computer operator which he thought would be good for me. I interviewed with the NASA Lead and, weeks later, was offered the position, which I accepted. However, before I could report to work, I got sick again, and was hospitalized for two months. I got out less than two weeks before my wedding date of April 15, so it was a very stressful time.

I had started passing gallstones, which may have been what triggered it this time. They recommended removing my gallbladder, but I refused, concerned that having the surgery would delay my return and I was worried because I still hadn't reported to my new job. However, Dick telephoned me to see how I was doing and assured me that I didn't have to worry about my new job, that I just needed to concentrate on getting well. Even if the new position didn't hold out, he said, I would still have my job with Nimbus. I was hugely relieved and could now focus more on my recovery and my impending wedding date the following month.

My doctor advised me that my best shot for being healthy for my wedding was to undergo the surgery then, rather than wait and be still passing stones when April 15 rolled around. He said the procedure was so standard now that I would probably be totally healed well ahead of time. So, I consented to have my gallbladder removed.

I woke up in recovery suffering intense abdominal pain and cried out for help. They gave me more pain meds, which mercifully knocked me out. When I awoke again, I was back in my hospital room and it was dark. This time the pain was manageable and I was able to tough it out.

Curious, I took a look and was surprised by how long the incision was. It began above my navel and extended all the way across to one side, where a drain tube poked out. At the time, I didn't know what it was.

After about a week they removed it. The doctor told me to hold onto the bed rails and take a deep breath. When he started pulling out the tube, I gasped. It was as if he were pulling out my organs as well. The tube was over a foot long and it felt like it took forever to come out—the pain took my breath away. I didn't ever want to see another drain tube again! They bandaged the hole as I composed myself. Thank God I had but one gallbladder to remove, I thought.

I was initially released from the hospital a couple of days later, in mid-March. They gave me instructions on how to change the dressing and clean the wound, which I did on the second day at home. I managed to do it well enough, but it bled. By the next evening I was in pain. Another crisis episode had begun, and by midnight we were headed back to D.C. The incision had become infected and I was hospitalized another two weeks, until the first week of April. I was so worried about getting well for my wedding that I believe it actually delayed my recovery. When I came out of the hospital, I had dropped nearly 25 pounds, from 136 to 112. I'd been fitted for my tuxedo before I'd been hospitalized, and so now they had to make some quick adjustments so it wasn't hanging off me. I had barely more than a week to get my strength back.

The night before our wedding, we held our rehearsal and then it was time for Shari and I to part company. Shari was staying with Vanessa, her maid of honor, and the rest of the girls in the wedding party. I was staying at home and Larry, my best man, was hanging with me. As we went our separate ways, the guys decided they wanted to continue partying. They headed off while Larry and I went back to change clothes. When we got to where they'd been headed, though, there was no sign of them. We started making calls. They were at Darryl's, we learned. But by the time we got there, they had left and were now at Matthew's house. We never did catch up with them, because by the time we got to Matthew's, they had headed off to D.C. to hit some of the strip clubs. Larry and I decided to call it a night and get some rest, probably the best thing I could have done, considering how weak I still was.

Chapter Nineteen

April 15, 1989

I awoke with joy in my heart, no fear or reservations. It was raining, and continued to rain the entire day, which I was assured was a sign of good luck. God's grace, more like it.

Larry and I got showered, shaved, and dressed. Carrying our jackets so as not to crease them, we headed for the church, arriving with plenty of time to spare. As my groomsmen arrived, we completed and fine-tuned our looks before the photographer arrived to take the pre-ceremony photographs.

Then, it was showtime. I was on cloud nine, and the ceremony was picture-perfect. My illness had meant we hadn't gotten all of the invitations out, but word of mouth went out that any of my family would be welcome, and to my delight, everyone came, showing me even more love than I had anticipated.

I stood at the altar, looking out at all the familiar faces before we got started. My aunts, uncles, cousins, nieces, nephews, and friends were beaming, as were all of Shari's family. I now knew every one of them. My sister-in-law Sonia was our coordinator and she was busy as a little bee, ushering everyone in on time.

Chapter Nineteen

Our parents Shari's grandmother were seated and my cousin Alex sang "Lady."

I watched as the bridal party, which included my beautiful baby Tina, who was just eleven, assembled at the back of the church and began their walk down the aisle as Alex and his sister Alice sang "Endless Love." Shari's godson and cousin David was our ring bearer and my niece Tanya was the flower girl.

By now, everyone was in place. The opening strains of "Here Comes the Bride" began as my eyes, glued to the door at the back of the church, widen when it swings open to reveal the love of my life, dressed in white, as beautiful as anything I'd ever seen in my life.

My eyes never left her as she walked down the aisle, and I could see her warm smile beneath her veil. I was mesmerized. When she reached my side, we turned to face Rev. Kess, but I could hardly keep my eyes off her. The pastor addressed us and I tried to pay attention to what he was saying. He spoke of how our bodies are no longer our own, and that we should always know where each other's body was, that we should never allow anyone to intrude in our marriage, and that, from this day forth, we would walk in unity with God and each other.

The ceremony was beautiful and my pastor seemed to have prayed extra intently for us. I was so grateful for the extra special care and attention he displayed on our day. When he pronounced us husband and wife and told me to kiss the bride, I was like a kid in a candy store. Our kiss was sweet, not too short and not too long.

As we walked down the aisle together, I exhaled in relief, feeling as if I had been holding my breath for the past hour. After most of the congregation had congratulated us and left, we went back into the sanctuary to take the first photos of the entire wedding party. After that, Shari and I climbed into our limo and headed off to the reception, toasting each other with a glass of sparkling cider.

The reception was at the Prince Georges Ballroom. It was classy, yet affordable. My Aunt Delores had agreed to cater the affair, so I knew the food would be great. My brother David and cousin Eddie were the DJ crew, with David announcing the arrival of the wedding party.

When Shari and I walked in, our welcome was warm and enthusiastic, a heady feeling. We had our first dance, and our first laugh as Shari's dad climbed under the table when the parents were called to join us out on the dance floor. After coaxing him to come out, we got our second chuckle as he joined his wife, with Mama Doris towering about a foot and a half over Papa Spoon's head. He took it like a champ and they completed their dance. During the dance, we swapped partners periodically, and now the laugh was on me as I danced with Vanessa. She was wearing her tall heels that day, putting my face at the same height as her boobs. The party was getting started now, and we were all just getting primed.

The videographer was a little goofy, and kept coming up with wacky things to do for photo opportunities. For example, on the dance floor, he had my groomsmen surround Shari and me, and had them take turns leaning in to kiss my bride on the cheek. And when we sat down for dinner, he asked each groomsman to go to the bridesmaid they'd escorted so he could film each of them feeding the other fruit from the fruit salad. I thought it looked kind of tacky, but it was too late to protest.

Chapter Nineteen

One more notable chuckle came at the end of the best man's toast. Larry spoke beautiful and inspiring words, but what proved hilarious was seeing my baby girl Tina take her first taste of Champagne. She spat the wine across the table. Note to self: Whenever having a toast involving an eleven-year-old, make sure what they're drinking is apple juice.

The cake was beautiful—at least initially. It collapsed and the lady who had baked it was so upset that she left early, with a headache. Still, it was absolutely delicious, with layers flavored with vanilla, piña colada, and amaretto. Regardless of what the videographer might have wanted, Shari and I had decided ahead of time that we wouldn't be smashing cake into each other's face.

Shari's friend Denise caught the bouquet and our buddy Daniel caught the garter. She was careful in letting him put the garter on her leg. All in all, everything was smooth sailing for the rest of the evening. By the time we left the reception and went to Michael's to change out of our wedding clothes, it was after 11:00 p.m. The house was packed with people as we said goodnight and headed for the penthouse suite at the Baltimore Harbor Hotel, a gift from Vanessa and Ron. We arrived not long before midnight. Despite our exhaustion, I did carry my wife over the threshold. When we entered the suite, we looked at each other in disbelief. The place was huge! We had three rooms, the main room, and smaller sitting room beyond that, which led to the bedroom. The first room featured a baby grand piano. It was like something out of the TV show *Lifestyles of the Rich and Famous*. One entire wall of the bedroom was totally glass, flanked by giant drapes, which provided a fantastic view of the harbor below and the city, ablaze with lights. I'd had no idea Baltimore could produce such a view.

(We found out the next day that celebrities normally stayed in that room, most recently actor/comedian Eddie Murphy.)

The bathroom featured his and her toilets, a walk-in shower, an immense bathtub, double sinks, and a shoe-shine machine. We were just sorry we hadn't gotten there earlier! We jumped into bed to consummate our marriage before the new day rolled in, then laid there, contentedly, in each other's arms, as if in a dream, and fell asleep looking out over the big city.

When we awoke, we agreed that we wouldn't vacate our room until checkout time and stayed in bed as late as we dared. We checked out and had a very late breakfast—brunch, really—and then went home to drop off our bags before heading over to Mike's to open our gifts. There were so many that we only opened a few before packing everything up to take home. We had arranged to take several days off to relax and enjoy ourselves as newlyweds before it was time to return to work. I was reporting to my new job at NASA.

Chapter Twenty

※

My NASA rep was a sweet, soft-spoken woman named Catherine whom everybody called Cat. We hit it off right from the start and I just couldn't thank her enough for waiting for me through my lengthy illness.

My company had transitioned from RCA to Martin Marietta and I now had a totally new management team. The Special Payloads Division turned out to be a great project to be involved in, and it was extremely popular when I joined it. Scientists, students, and various other groups were competing to have their science experiments transported onboard the space shuttles. I was running a computer room that housed an IBM mainframe hosting a UNIX/AIX operating system. I had no prior training in UNIX, but a young man named Tim showed me how to keep the facility running properly, taught me many of the UNIX commands, and showed me the instruction book nearby if I got stuck and needed to get into deeper troubleshooting. I studied the system hard every day to learn as much as I could. I wanted to instill total confidence in Cat that I was sufficiently skilled to handle the job before Tim moved on to his new position. In a short time, I had won her over and our relationship developed beyond mere boss and employee to confidants and friends.

Several weeks passed until the videographer delivered to us the wedding videotape. I watched it and was appalled and deeply disappointed. It was the most amateurish piece of work I had ever seen. The tape would play and suddenly, mid-scene, it would jump skip to another scene, which was made even more glaringly evident because of how the music that was being played would shift mid-song. Our wedding ceremony was about thirty minutes in length and I was eager to watch it unfold as a member of the audience this time. Instead, the videographer had repeatedly paused the recording while he changed his position and the result was jerky and staccato, without even the opportunity to hear the various songs sung through to completion. I chided myself for not having checked the guy's credentials and references. At least the day itself had gone flawlessly, Shari reminded me. That's what was important.

So, despite the video debacle, Shari and I appeared to be off to a perfect start. Along with our friends Vanessa and Ron, and Larry and Debra, who'd gotten married the previous year, one week apart, we celebrated together and were all enjoying our new lives. And being married didn't signal an end to our partying and playing softball, volleyball, and bowling, which would continue for years to come.

The only shadow was that my sickle cell crisis episodes were growing in frequency. Episodes didn't vary in intensity—they were always excruciating and often unbearable—but are classified simply in terms of how long the episode lasted. Sometimes I would bounce back in a week while other times it would drag on for as much as two months. One time, after having been in the hospital for about two weeks, and suffering relentless agony the entire time, Shari brought Vanessa on one of her visits. They asked how I was, but when I tried to answer, I burst into tears, bawling uncontrollably like a baby. Shari lunged for the call button and the nurse appeared and gave me my overdue pain meds. I was embarrassed because if there was one thing I had learned to do early on, it was to exert strict self-control out of necessity, because anything—fear, excitement, overexertion, anxiety, even plain old sadness—could trigger a crisis. I'd make myself smile all of the time, no matter what situation I faced. (In fact, a couple of times, that ability to smile through adversity got me in trouble when bosses chewed me out about something. I just stood there smiling, trying not to get upset, but one guy took offense and demanded to know why I was smiling. I wiped the smile off my face, knowing he wouldn't understand if I explained it, and let him finish his rant. As soon as he turned and walked away, that determined smile returned to my face. God, not he, was in control of my life.)

Cat and I had progressed to having long talks about whatever was happening in our lives. When I would get sick again and be absent for weeks, even months, she always greeted me with a smile and a hug when I came back.

With the episodes increasing in frequency and severity, I was determined to avoid St. Agnes Hospital and had Shari take me the next time to Northwest Hospital Center, which was actually closer to home. They treated me well but still lacked the necessary experts in sickle cell anemia, so I couldn't get the care I needed.

Shari sat with me most of the time, whether I was awake or not. One afternoon, I heard that same voice I'd heard once before.

"I love you, and I'll never leave you."

I sat up and looked around but there was no one there. I chalked it up to my imagination again and soon forgot about it.

As no other hospital matched Howard University Hospital in terms of sickle cell expertise, Shari and I agreed that future hospital stays would be best done there. However, there was no sign of Dr. Castro or Dr. Perlin, another doctor who had successfully treated me, by now, and that was reflected in the service I received.

One time I was put in a room with some guy who'd come from the psych ward. He was tied to either his bed or a chair, and was always working to free himself from his restraints. I awoke on a Friday night, emerging from the effects of my medication only to see this big hand by my side table. Apparently, a nurse had come in while I was sleep and instead of waking me to take my meds, she left the dose on the bedside table. My roommate had managed to work himself loose, scoot across the floor in his chair, and was handing me the pills.

"Take your medicine!" he ordered, his voice loud, his tone aggressive.

"What are you doing? Just put it down. I'll get it later." I didn't want to take the pills after he'd handled them. I closed my eyes, focusing on the pain that had returned.

Thwack!

I shrieked, agonizing pain shooting through me. The guy had just walloped me across my legs.

"I said, take your medicine!" he roared.

I started yelling for help, all the while desperately pushing the call button.

Chapter Twenty

"Get away from me!" I shouted. I felt a flicker of relief when he scooted back across the floor to his bedside. Still, no one had responded to my calls for help.

Knowing the guy was psycho, I grabbed the only item nearby that had any heft to it—the old telephone on the bedside table, figuring I could split his head open with it if he came back and tried to assault me again.

I must have passed out, because the next thing I knew, a nurse woke me up during the night and asked why I was clutching the phone to my chest. I told her what had happened and that she needed to move one of us into another room immediately. She half-chuckled in sympathy and said she would see what they could do.

Nothing happened. I kept the phone in my hand until the next morning. My roommate kept to his side of the room, but there was no sign of any room change being organized. After breakfast, someone arrived to help me get washed and changed. Exhausted, I dozed fitfully in and out for a while. It was a Saturday morning and I wasn't expecting anyone to come see me so early, but Vanessa's husband Ron appeared shortly before noon and sat with me.

All of a sudden there was a flurry of activity. Several nurses darted into the room and started hastily packing up the other man's things.

"Mr. Collins, we're moving your roommate out right now. You'll be able to relax and get some good rest now."

I was puzzled for a moment and then it hit me. Ron was six-foot-five, white, and wearing a suit jacket. They must have seen him striding down the hall and into my room and thought he was my lawyer.

We watched as they rolled him back upstairs to the psych ward, where he clearly should have remained.

I looked at Ron.

"I'm going to call you whenever things aren't going well, as I know now that once you appear, my problems will be over." We laughed and my day was all the better for it.

Chapter Twenty-One

Shari and I had been married for eight months when we headed back home to the Eastern Shore for a New Year's gathering with my family, which turned out to be a wonderful time.

The next morning, we were all cleaning up when Shari commented on how hot the house was.

"No it's not!" several people exclaimed and we all laughed.

I looked at her, amused, and then hesitated. She was indeed what I would describe as glowing. My eyes widened.

"Baby, you are pregnant!"

"No I'm not!" she insisted. She looked at me, hesitantly. "You think so?"

Everybody burst out laughing. I grinned.

"Yes, dear, I can see it all over you."

When we got back home to Baltimore, we swung past the store to pick up a home pregnancy test. Sure enough, we were "with child." We were both ecstatic.

As time went by though, my spells of illness were becoming more frequent. I wondered if it were because I was feeling stressed by the prospect of bringing a baby into the world and not having the opportunity to see him or her grow up. My biggest fear, which

I'd shared with Shari, was that it wasn't perhaps a good idea to have children when there was a very real risk that they would inherit the sickle cell gene and end up sick, like me. She had gotten tested before we got engaged and assured me that she had no trace of sickle cell, no sign of any blood anomaly.

"You're not getting rid of me," she'd say, whenever I expressed concern. I had fallen more and more in love with her each passing day, so much so that I couldn't imagine life without her anymore.

I'd always respond, "I'm not going anywhere." There was no turning back for either of us in our relationship, but always in the back of my mind was the fact that, for sickle cell sufferers, like me and my brother, they rarely ever reached adulthood. We had at least dodged that bullet. I found comfort in my faith that only God controlled my fate: when doctors say no, my God can say yes, and He always has the final word.

On September 21, 1990, Brittany Marie Collins was born. Our beautiful little girl was here and we were just so excited.

The doctor discovered that Brittany had one foot that turned in and after a couple of weeks he fitted her with special shoes and a brace that forced her feet into alignment. As time went by, her feet turned out to be ok, but it was both odd and funny, watching her adapt to the brace. She had to wear it so long that she began to crawl while still wearing the brace. It was amazing how fast she began to move around despite her feet being locked into the brace.

Before she started walking, the doctor declared that the brace could come off, and she began to walk by the time she was ten months old.

During this time, my older daughter Tina and I were still pretty close and we would talk and send little messages to each other. She seemed to be just fine with the idea of having a new sister, but her mom became a little nervous that Tina would no longer get the support that she was entitled to, so she decided to file for child support as a legal option. I didn't agree with it at the time, and I told her that I liked having them call and ask me for things because it kept us in touch. I felt that if she were getting support through the mail every week, then we would lose touch because they might think they had no reason to call and talk to me.

Still, Sasha's mind was made up, so off to court we went, I underwent the required paternity test, and Tina was established as belonging to me. I was actually relieved to receive confirmation of this, because there had been many rumors through the years about whether I was actually her father.

The court process was otherwise still pretty stressful. I was nervous about showing up without a lawyer but really didn't have the money to bring one down to Princess Anne with me and I would never trust one from there with any part of my life. So there I was, sitting in the courtroom, listening to all of the different cases involving child custody and support, amazed at the severity and harshness of the rulings going out that were never in favor of the men. Guys were being thrown into jail or ordered to pay such a high percentage of their income that it would be impossible for them to be able to pay rent and electric with what was left.

The unthinkable unfolded before me as this young black guy was brought before the judge for not fulfilling his child support order. The young lady on the other side with the baby was white, and I just flushed with fear and compassion for what was about to happen to this young man. He was definitely in the wrong town. The judge immediately raised the amount he was to pay and gave him sixty days in jail to think about it. That's when I decided that I really should not be there without a lawyer.

My thoughts were racing a mile a minute as I tried to figure out how to get my case delayed. Just as I got up to go to the clerk's office, an official called my name. I followed him down the hall and into an office where Sasha and the state's attorney were waiting. I handed my income statements over to the clerk and they start calculating what I should be paying. The figure is nearly a hundred dollars a week, and I say that is impossible for me to do.

At the time I was making around $300 per week after taxes, insurance, and deductions. I was already carrying Tina on my medical insurance and I was up to my neck in medical bills, which I had proof of with me. My wife's income was the only way we could afford to pay our rent. I had been getting so sick lately that I was missing up to a month or two of income at any given moment, so when they asked me what I thought I could pay, I said $35 per week. The state's attorney went ballistic! He started ranting about how we could just march in to see the judge right then and there, and that they didn't have to accommodate me because I made too much money as it was.

"Ok," I said. "I'll go before the judge."

"Oh no!" Sasha cried, alarmed for me. "You don't want to do that!"

"No, I don't want to," I agreed, "and I won't go in there today. We can reschedule and I'll come back with a lawyer. If I have to pay that much I might as well quit my job and let the system take care of my other child too."

Sasha turned to the state's attorney.

"I'll take what he's offering."

Once again the state's attorney went on a tirade and I found myself wondering whether we were still focused on what was best for Tina or was he thinking he had a black man working at NASA, probably making more than many white men in Princess Anne, Maryland, did, but we signed the agreement and were free to go.

The child support order went directly to my employer and was automatically deducted from my check each week and deposited in Sasha's account. I was grateful to Sasha and impressed that she cared enough about me not to let them drag me through the fire the way I could have been. I'm not sure I ever told her that I was grateful or said a simple thank you, however, which I deeply regret.

Sure enough, once the formal child support was in effect, I began to hear less and less from Tina. When I could no longer reach her at all, I learned that they had moved. And no one could tell me where.

Chapter Twenty-Two

Unfortunately, my health continued to decline and I missed six months of our baby's first year, as well as any contact with Tina. I was in and out of the hospital a month here, two months there—the entire month of February, for example, and then back in again by Memorial Day.

That Memorial Day weekend, we had decided to visit Shari's aunts and uncles in Norfolk and Chesapeake for the holiday. We arrived on the Saturday afternoon and within moments of our arrival, I spun into crisis. I was later told that I must have already been suffering with asymptomatic sickle cell chest syndrome, but the pain only began when I got to Norfolk. It came on so quickly, so intensely, that I was hustled off to the hospital within a half hour of our arrival. I had double pneumonia as a further complication and the doctors didn't know how to treat me. If they treated the pneumonia, it would aggravate the sickle cell, and vice versa.

After a day or two the doctor managed to reach Dr. Castro at Howard University Hospital. They discussed my case, and because I was in such agony, they decided to put me in a medically induced coma to give my body a chance to recover. I'm not totally sure how long I was out, but I think it was about two weeks.

Chapter Twenty-Two

When I awoke, I felt better, but my lungs were still congested. I began massage therapy, every other day or so, and slowly responded with improved lung capacity. As my oxygen intake improved, the crisis became more bearable, but I was still in trouble for the next two months. Shari had to go home with Brittany, alone and worried, and returned on the weekends. I didn't see my baby the entire time because I didn't want Shari to bring her into the hospital in case she contracted some nasty virus, or worse.

Weekdays, Shari's family and those of my cousins who lived in the area would stop in and check on me. Aunt Kitten and Aunt Ernestine, Shari's cousins Courtney and Shelby, and my cousins Charles, Elaina and Mike all did their best to make sure that I didn't get too lonely. By the time I got out of the hospital it was the end of July and I felt like I was in a strange land as I rode home. My mom and dad had picked me up in the middle of the week and taken me to their house; Shari would come on the weekend to take me home. It felt so surreal to walk into my childhood house in Princess Anne after so long. The big thrill was when Shari and Brittany arrived on the weekend to take me back to our house in Baltimore. I can't describe the joy in my heart when they walked through the door. I wish I could say that was the last time that I would have to spend another two months in the hospital, but it wasn't.

By this time, baby Brittany was walking and getting into everything. She loved hiding out in the closet in the dark, which fascinated me. Whenever I would hunt her down, she would laugh so hard. She reminded me a lot of Tina in that she seemed so happy all of the time but she wouldn't tolerate anyone but Shari, Mom Doris, or me handling her. Everyone wanted to hold her and get to know her but she would scream, twist, and pull away.

My sister Belinda volunteered to bring her down to Mom and Dad's to spend the weekend with her grandparents. Brittany screamed from the time she was strapped into her seat all the way there, over two hours, and by the time they arrived, Belinda was a wreck. She vowed that Brittany would never be allowed in her car ever again. (Through all the years, she never broke that vow, although I have little doubt that in a critical situation she would have caved. She insists she wouldn't have, but says it with a smile.)

I managed to stay out of the hospital throughout the entire month of August, but by September I was back in again. As usual, it was an excruciating event, but this time things were different. Much of the time I was dazed, completely out of it. I had no sense of the passage of time, or days, and I only awoke when the pain meds had worn off, leaving me in agony.

Even the doctors treated me differently this time, mentioning things I had never heard before, like liver and kidney function. They couldn't control my high fever, and my blood pressure, which had always been ideal before, was now dangerously high. They were worried that I might have a heart attack or stroke.

My legs were so swollen with edema that my knees essentially disappeared. They looked like tree trunks going straight down instead of curved legs. My arms were swollen as well and the IVs kept having to be redone. The fluids and meds they were trying to pump into me seemed to be just pooling under my skin instead of circulating through me. They ran out of places to put the IV and were talking about running it up through my groin, but that was where I drew the line.

By now I was exhausted to my core and I had resolved that I probably wasn't going to emerge from this episode. One night

I called Shari and told her that I couldn't go on, and that I was ready to go home. It terrified her and she began to cry and plead with me to hold on. She said that she would be there first thing in the morning, and that she wanted to see my smile.

When we hung up, she immediately called my sister Vernetta, in pieces. Vernetta assured her that I would be ok and that she just had to remain positive about it. Afterward, Vernetta called me immediately and asked me why I was upsetting my wife so much.

"I'm tired. I don't think I have the strength to endure this any longer, to fight it anymore. I've made my peace with it. Vernetta, I'm ready to go. All that I ask of God is to let my brothers be saved in my passing."

"I have news for you, my dear brother. Jesus already died for them and you can't be in His shoes because He overcame for everyone, including you. God's not through with you yet, so you just hold onto His hand."

Her words hit home, and gave me new insight into what God's plan might be for each of us. Unlike us, He doesn't see us through human eyes but through divine eyes, as only God can.

The next morning Shari was there bright and early, a concerned look on her face, but when she saw me staring back at her, without any look of hopelessness or fatigue, her expression changed and she threw her arms around me, tears in her eyes.

"I'm sorry," I murmured. "I didn't mean to upset you."

"Don't ever do that to me again," she said, holding me tightly.

Despite my change of heart, the next two weeks passed with no improvement in my condition. Instead, I continued to deteriorate. The doctors ordered repeated blood and urine tests, warning me that my kidneys were shutting down and my liver function was poor. The edema was also getting worse, and I was aware that I was looking more and more like a swollen blob every day. Doctors would visit in groups now, instead of singly, and discuss my case among themselves.

One evening I was half asleep when I became aware of what sounded like a team of doctors in my room, having a solemn discussion. I refrained from opening my eyes so I could listen to them talk openly. A nurse came in to check my IV bags as the doctors were leaving and one of them turned to her.

"Give him whatever he asks for. If he wants pain meds, just give them to him—don't worry about the timing. Just keep him comfortable."

My eyes were still closed. Had they given up on me? It certainly sounded like it. Clearly, there was nothing else they could think of to do.

I lay there the rest of the evening, worrying that if I went back to sleep, I might not wake up. I decided not to call Shari, not wanting to upset her again. It would be better, I thought, if God wanted to take me home that He did it without her finding out until after I was gone.

Inevitably, I began to doze, drifting in and out of sleep, when I awoke, but I wasn't in my hospital room. Was I dreaming? Because I never remember my dreams when I wake up, yet everything was so vivid, so brilliant, so detailed and clear that surely it must be a dream.

I am sitting at the table in my mom's kitchen, and my mom is standing at the stove, cooking. Without warning, an invisible force snatches me up and slams me against the wall. Before I slide to the floor, it picks me up again and slams me against another wall. The pain on impact is brutal.

"Somebody help me!" I scream. "Please!" My mother is watching helplessly in horror, weeping, as I scream for help. The force continues to lift me up before I can touch the floor and slam me against wall after wall. It is trying to destroy me, and I continue to shriek for help, but no one comes.

Fragments of my life flash before me, brushes with death—the numerous car accidents, the mob attack on Eddie and Jack that left me miraculously unscathed—as the pain of each impact shudders through my body.

The final throw hurls me not against a wall but past my mother and through the window above the kitchen sink. But instead of hitting the ground outside, I shoot straight up into the air.

"Lord Jesus, help me!" I cry.

Abruptly, the trajectory halts and I am hanging, motionless, in mid-air.

"I told you that I love you and I'll never leave you."

I recognize the voice immediately.

"All you had to do was call Me. It wasn't Me trying to kill you."

I knew suddenly that I was in a special, protected place, in the presence of The Almighty.

As this realization settles into me, I'm immediately transported into my parents' living room, enveloped in peaceful calm and tranquility, contemplating what has just happened.

The living room fades and I am engulfed in a pure white fog so thick that I can't see the hands I'm holding up in front of my face. Slowly, the fog dissipates to reveal the all too familiar hospital room.

I found myself lying back in bed, the last wisps of fog vanishing, filled with awe at what just happened. That was no dream, I thought. That was a vision. It was as if God had been the mist, initially blocking every other distraction from my awareness. When it disappeared, my surroundings seemed dull, as if I'd shifted from a vivid color film to one in faded black and white.

I lay there, replaying it over and over in my head until a nurse entered my room. Seeing me awake, she murmurs, "Good morning," as if mindful of what the doctors have warned her about letting me rest comfortably.

I look out the window. It's daybreak. She takes my blood pressure. She hesitates, looking at the dial, and jots it down. Then she takes my temperature. She looks at the thermometer and then gives me a disbelieving look.

"How do you feel?"

I pause. I'm not sure how to answer her because I'm not sure how I feel. Confused, I swiftly inventory my physical state and it dawns on me what's different. I'm not in any pain. I'm not feverish; I'm not chilled. I look at her.

"I… I think I'm ok actually."

"Your temperature is 98.6," she says, and her smile meets mine.

She puts a reassuring hand on my shoulder before hurrying out of the room. It's Saturday, when I don't typically see a doctor.

Breakfast arrives and I discover I'm hungry. I sit up and eat and then gingerly get out of bed and head to the bathroom where I get washed. It feels good to put on a fresh gown, to be doing all of this without assistance for a change.

Shari arrives and looks astonished to see me sitting up, eating lunch. I chuckle out loud at her expression. Her eyes and her smile widen and I can sense her relief, her whole body relaxing.

The rest of the weekend flew by in a blur. The doctor came by on Sunday, but made no comment about the change in my condition. In the past, my improvements were always slow and reasonably steady. I don't ever recall feeling so much stronger so quickly, but by Monday, they discharged me. The doctor did express concern that my kidney and liver functions were still of great concern, and cautioned me to return if things started to go downhill again. He arranged for me to return for a follow-up appointment in about ten days. I rolled out of Howard University Hospital feeling better and more energetic than I had ever felt after one of my episodes.

By Wednesday, I felt well enough to venture out to our church's prayer service. When I appeared, everyone greeted me delightedly. We all knelt at the altar and took turns raising our praises, petitions, and concerns before the Lord. When it was my turn, I thanked God for what He had once again brought me through and for allowing me to see yet another day.

Unbeknownst to me, our pastor, Rev. Kess, had entered the back of the church as I had begun my prayer. We wrapped up the prayer session and became aware of some commotion behind us. People were consoling the pastor who was praising God more and more animatedly, tears streaming down his face.

Regaining his composure, he made his way toward us, to the front of the church, and explained what had just happened.

Looking at me, he said that he had visited me in the hospital on several occasions, and each time found me unresponsive. He would pray for me and then quietly slip out. The last time, he said, he was left wondering—doubting—whether he would ever see me alive again. He had been unprepared, upon walking in, to see me kneeling at the altar, thanking God for one more day, and had been abruptly filled with indescribable joy and gratitude.

A young lady named Geneva approached the sanctuary, where we were standing, and confessed that she had been sitting in the back, struggling with something she felt the Lord wanted her to do. *Lord, I can't do it—I can't tell him that*, she kept thinking. When God did not give her peace, she prayed, "Lord, if this is truly You, then please give me a sign." It was at that precise moment that Rev. Kess shared what had come over him upon seeing me, and she felt compelled to tell me what God wanted her to say. She looked me in the eye.

"God told me to tell you that you are healed."

I was momentarily speechless. Everyone froze for a split second as they absorbed her words. I flash back to the vision I'd had in the hospital and how that marked the dramatic improvement in my condition. My mind flicked past other strange, sometimes miraculous incidents that had occurred in my life. It would appear that God did indeed have a plan for me that would not culminate now, in a hospital bed.

I looked at her, gravely, as all of this soaked into me.

"I accept that," I said. The group surrounded me and began to pray and praise God for the great news that we had received. From that moment forth I walked into my future as a healed man of God, determined to give Him honor, praise and glory, every day.

Chapter Twenty-Two

For the next year it seemed as though the devil tested me relentlessly. I had to pray and rebuke the Enemy constantly. Without warning, I would feel the familiar stabs of pain and immediately pray and recall to the Lord that He said I was healed. Instead of lying down or reaching for my medicine, I continued doing whatever I had been doing and the pain would fade.

There were times that I would open the Bible and search for passages on healing. The quickest way, I soon learned, to put the Enemy to flight was to start reciting what is now one of my favorite passages, Isaiah 53:5:

> *But He was wounded for our transgressions, He was bruised for our iniquities: the chastisement for our peace was upon Him; and by His stripes we are healed.*

Another, one that confirms Isaiah's words, is 1 Peter 2:24:

> *Who Himself bore our sins in His own body on the tree, that we, having died to sins, might live for righteousness — by whose stripes you were healed.*

The first passage says "with his stripes we *are* healed" and the latter one says "by whose stripes you *were* healed," in the past tense. That means it is finished. Already done.

If I have learned anything, I know that "God's promises are always and forever true." So I have cited these scriptures for years, and after a while, the Enemy gave up trying to convince me that I had not been healed. After several years, the pain never returned.

Chapter Twenty-Three

※

At work Cat and I were thriving. There is nothing about the IBM mainframe that I had not mastered, and she has total confidence that I can manage the system with or without her. She rejoiced greatly with me when I told her about my healing, and we began counting the years from that rebirth and celebrating together.

My racing days were pretty much done by that time, because I was more focused on being a family man and a man of God. We had learned a few lessons with Brittany who not only had been saddled with braces on her feet but had developed colic, which left her screaming every night until 3:00 a.m. for over a month. We tried everything, from changing her formula to using anti-gas medicines and putting Karo corn syrup in her water bottle.

Some of it seemed to help, but the best remedy was always my straddling her over my right arm, like I was carrying a football tucked against my side, and walking, while gently rocking her until she fell asleep. That helped her sleep best, although it wasn't ideal for me when I had to get up at 6:00 a.m. to go to work.

With Shari working rotating shifts, she wasn't always aware of what we went through, but she was a real trouper when she was home. We would work together and take turns rocking and walking.

We had the added advantage of a little church mother, Mrs. Shirley Lomax, who took Shari and me under her wing and shared countless pieces of wisdom with us about parenting and protecting our babies. Ms. Shirley was a loving and nurturing elder of Queen's Chapel, and she was very straightforward when she wanted you to know something. She didn't believe in sugarcoating things, but she was never just plain rude either. She was a mother, first and always.

On our arrival to church each Sunday, she always came over to inspect how we were traveling. She would tell us, or show us, how she wanted us to wrap or swaddle the baby. She would tell us to never let the baby be exposed to the air when going outside for the first six weeks. Through her tips, our children after Brittany sailed through without any problems. I learned a lot from Ms. Shirley, and we weren't the only beneficiaries of her knowledge and wisdom.

Even so, I took pride in the feeling that I belonged to her and she belonged to me, no matter what. She brought us home for Sunday dinner and welcomed me in when I would stop by after work and hang out, waiting for the Male Chorus rehearsals.

It was one of those afternoons that she turned me into a fried-liver-and-onions maniac. I had never eaten liver so tender and delicious in my entire life. Mr. Lomax, affectionately known as Brother, was the director of our choir and the entire family welcomed everyone they met. They would feed anyone, anytime or anywhere. It wasn't unusual for us to stop by and have a snack before rehearsal and sometimes we would gather again after rehearsal and have a full meal with them.

Chapter Twenty-Three

I had joined the Male Chorus back when I was still experiencing bouts of sickness. Rev. Kess had a brother with whom I often sat during service, unless he was performing with the choir. He also recorded every program the choir attended, as well as most of all the other choirs in the church. I was absolutely mesmerized by the Male Chorus. They were about thirty-six strong in number and the sound was just heavenly. They sounded as good as any recording artists in the business and, to me, they were celebrities.

Ed invited me one day to come and sit in on the rehearsals, and said I would be surprised at how easily I would fit in. Ed was a big jokester and I loved his sense of humor, but he wasn't kidding about this. The guys took me in and I built a special relationship with each and every one of them. We traveled to someone else's church every weekend, be it Saturday or Sunday. The group was so popular that we stayed booked over a year in advance. I would often be missing for months but they always welcomed me and helped get me back up to speed with the songs. Sometimes they would visit me when I was hospitalized, even though I might not have been aware of their presence.

Now that I was healed, I prayed for God to heal others who were in need. Butch, a choir member, was anointed with the gift of song like no one that I had ever met. He could sing anything and everything, and the Holy Spirit just rode the airwaves around him. When he sang "The Love of God," or "His Eye is on the Sparrow," I would often lose track of the chorus part because I was caught up in the spirit. Sadly, Butch became ill before I was healed and by the time God freed me, Butch was diagnosed with stage IV cancer. He fought with everything he had inside and traveled with us as much as he could. The last time he sang with us we had traveled to Norfolk, Virginia, and he used a cane to get around. I watched him stand with us, leaning on that cane, as he belted out the most wonderful version of "His Eye is on the Sparrow." Everyone was shouting with joy and he was so exhausted that he had to return to the bus and lie down immediately afterward, while we continued with the program. That was the last trip he took with us. I was healed shortly after that, but I never got to tell him about the miracle. He was gone about a month after I got healed, and the choir was just devastated. He had sung lead on about fifty songs during his time with the group and there was just no replacing him. The choir would go on, and God still blessed us with many talented voices, so we still stood out as an elite group of choristers. Memories of Samuel (Butch) Dodson are always with us, no matter where we go.

Around this same period, Vanessa's older sister Doreen, a sweet young lady with a heart of gold, had also fallen victim to cancer. She would do anything for anybody and never ask for anything in return. I had gotten to know her as I traveled around with Shari and Vanessa, and I was treated like family. I always regretted that I didn't get to tell her about my miracle as well. At the time, I was convinced that things could have been different, had they just known what was possible through God. It wasn't yet clear to me that God can heal in many different ways, including through death. When you have your name written in The Lamb's Book of Life, it is truly ok if God takes you to a place you can call home, where there is no more dying, no more pain, and no more struggles. I can tell you with all certainty that heaven is for real, and because of that, I'm not about to doubt that hell is also.

Chapter Twenty-Three

Shari and I had our hands full with Brittany when we learned our second baby was on the way. Brittany was just two years old and into everything. It was like running track to keep up with her. We were constantly saying, "No, don't bother that," or "No, don't touch that."

Most of the time that was just a signal for her to hurry up and get it done before we could get to her. I used to get so mad at her that I started spanking her, but it did no good. She had to have it her way and nothing else would do. She was absolutely crazy over sugar and would search every corner of the house, looking for candy. I generally knew when she found something to get into, because it got real quiet. That was my cue to get up and go find her. She just loved to hide out in small, dark spaces, so that meant the closets. I had already put child locks on the cabinets so she wouldn't get into the chemicals or cleaners. Even the pots and pans were on lockdown. I usually found her giggling in one of the bedroom closets, and occasionally the one in the living room. That one was stuffed so tightly already that she usually couldn't close the door, so it wasn't a favorite spot. When I would open the door, there she would be, with this huge grin on her face. Rarely, she would be playing with one of her favorite toys; usually it was food or candy that she sought. We had to be ever vigilant to not put down anything that could be potentially harmful in any way.

So now, with baby number two on the way, I didn't know what to expect. As before, my wife had the beautiful glow and not one day of morning sickness. She absolutely loved being pregnant, and I just loved to observe her as she progressed through the months. Mom Doris was just loving her grandmother role, and since Ms. Shirley was her neighbor, friend, Vanessa's mom, and our sitter for

Brittany, she would go over and pick her up from daycare as often as she could. She and Pop Jerome would watch over her with all the love and care in the world.

One morning I awoke to find Shari sitting on the side of the bed, rubbing her stomach and rocking. I knew immediately what was happening and asked how long she had been up.

"About an hour or two."

I leaped to my feet, grabbed my watch, and timed her contractions. They were less than five minutes apart.

"We've got to go," I said.

I got Brittany up, put her coat on, and strapped her into her car seat and took it and Shari's bag and put them in the car. Then I called Mom Doris and told her we were on our way to drop off Brittany, before helping Shari out to the car.

As we headed into the city, Shari sat quietly, rubbing her stomach in a wide circular motion. My gaze bounced between her and the traffic, not paying much attention to the speedometer. My attention was jerked to the rearview mirror when blue and red lights flashed behind me, less than a mile from Mom's house. The police officer approached my door and I rolled down the window.

"Sir, do you know how fast you were driving?" Before I could respond, he noticed Shari sitting there, rubbing this huge belly, and he says, "Oh."

"Yes sir, we're on our way to the hospital."

He waved me on and I pulled out. When we arrived at Mom and Poppa Spoon's house, I leaped out of the car with Brittany and handed her off to Mom, who was standing at the gate. That's when I noticed the police officer had followed me and was parked, watching, at the corner.

Chapter Twenty-Three

As I darted back to the car he pulled up beside me and said, "Follow me," and headed off toward the hospital, lights and siren rolling. It was kind of fun, racing in the wake of a speeding police car.

When we arrived at the hospital, the officer ran inside and came back with a wheelchair, and rolled Shari into the emergency room while I went to park. By the time I returned, he was gone. I never had a chance to thank him or even find out his name to report his good deed.

Brooke was born just thirty minutes after reaching the hospital. The anesthesiologist didn't even arrive on time. She delivered Brooke totally without meds, and she kept such good composure that I was amazed. Brooke was a beautiful little butterball, the complete opposite of Brittany. She was never colicky or as mischievous as her sister. She was calm and quiet and appeared content with just trying to keep up with her sister, following her everywhere she went. With Brittany into everything though, it wasn't always good to have Brooke trying to follow close behind.

She did get a few bruises involving her bigger sister, such as one instance we turned our backs and Brittany tried to pick her up from the bed. We heard a thump and turned around to find Brooke lying on the floor and Brittany trying to scoop her up again. She had a small bump on the head afterward, but stopped crying and began to smile and play almost immediately. And one day, when she was in her walker, Brittany and her cousin Adam were playing, running through the house. Brooke was trying to keep up with them and at some point they decided to go down to the basement. They left the door open and Brooke headed right behind them. We heard the sound of something falling down the stairs and our hearts sank as we dashed for the basement door. Brooke lay at the bottom of the steps, still in her walker, and miraculously right side up. She was crying, but she didn't have a scratch on her. We had to constantly drill big sis on how to look out for her little sister.

Chapter Twenty-Four

After working with Booty and the mainframe for almost five years, my managers began to pull me over to the main office at the corporate park. They needed some extra computer skills over there, because they were building a brand-new network throughout the facility. I split my day between Goddard and Forbes Boulevard, and became acquainted with a gentleman named Lee. He was the jewel in our new division of Lockheed Martin, following the merger of two companies, Lockheed and Martin Marietta. He was extremely bright and a no-nonsense kind of guy, yet always fair and kind. He had the kind of personality that commanded respect, but was still extremely easy to talk to.

He introduced me to two of his engineers and asked me to work with them to try to figure out why the brand new network would not go live. They walked me around the facility, showing me all that they had done and relaying their expectations. I had no experience at this time with what was called Thin Net BNC, but they frequently referred to a book on it, so that afternoon I picked up the book and took it home with me. That evening I sat down and went through the book. It was as if God had laid it all out in front of me.

This type of network depended on a signal to mark the end of a segment, after which it channeled all traffic back to the router or switch. Each line required a tiny tool at the end of the segment, called a terminator. The next day, Lee asked if I had figured it out yet.

"Yes sir, I believe that I have."

He leaped up from his desk and said, "Show me what you have."

We went to see the two engineers and I asked if they had a terminator. They handed me one and as we walked out to one of the network segments, I explained that each segment of the network was required to have a terminator installed that would signal back to the server the end and total length of the segment. There was also a limit as to how long a segment could be to function properly. We got to the end of a segment and I plugged in the terminator. The network on that segment went live immediately.

We proceeded to place terminators at the end of each segment and was rewarded when every line responded with valid network traffic. We were thankfully within the length limits on every segment. Lee looked at me, his expression serious.

"You're in charge of the new network. I'm going to let these guys return to their normal duties."

He went back to his office, got on his computer which now had great internet service, and found a class on network troubleshooting, which was being held at a hotel near Baltimore–Washington International Airport and signed me up. The location was ideal for me because it was right on the route I took to work every day.

It was a three-day course and had a ton of useful information that I was able to apply when I returned to work. As I went through the daily tasks of trying to secure our network and set up the permissions for users, I realized I was still out of my depth, so Lee agreed to bring in a temporary network administrator to custom train me on our system until I could handle everything comfortably.

What began as a great idea, during which I learned many of the basics of being a system administrator, or sys admin, soon raised concerns in me. I became aware that my temp trainer was performing more in-depth operations when I wasn't around. I was now assembling and upgrading computer hardware for the users and could install motherboards, memory, hard drives, network interface cards, floppy drives, and CD Rom drives, which kept me busy and on the move, but it appeared that my network trainer might have his mind set on becoming a permanent fixture and so to increase his perceived value, he wasn't sharing everything I needed to know with me. I needed to take a more direct approach in order to learn about the areas where I still needed training. So, whenever I caught him working at the server console, I would ask him specific questions about things I needed help in understanding. He was reluctant to be too forthcoming, but he also knew that answering my questions was the primary reason he was there, so he gave me proper answers that held up under my testing. Still, I had to fight hard to get straight answers and began to get irritated.

One day I came to work to find everyone walking around in a panic, some even in tears. Our contract at Special Payloads had been up for rebid and we'd lost it. The rest of the week, people were calling in to be excused from work and running after new job leads. The place was in total chaos, but I went about my daily activities as if nothing had changed.

For the next three months the company that had won the contract we'd lost was calling people in for interviews, and many were just leaving on their own. The guy who was supposed to be training me moved on to greener pastures after the first week. I thought that it was kind of odd that no one from the new company ever called me for an interview or even inquired about my position. I guess I wasn't needed, because they were not using our facility for the continuation of the project. They had their own location. Still I pressed on with the tasks at hand. Management was having me inventory all the hardware and packing items to be shipped out. They began to sell off the computers and furniture to other vendors and current employees. The goal was to clear out the entire facility for a new branch of Lockheed Martin to move in. As the facility got closer to closing, some members affiliated with the incoming project began to show up. It was at this time that I met Jim. He was a kind gentleman with an infectious laugh, and he knew exactly what he needed to get done. I worked with him for a couple of weeks, showing him the existing setup of the network and the layout of the building. I helped him get the facility ready for the Vision Two Thousand team connected to the Hubble Space Telescope Project. During the last week before my project was due to close out, Jim spoke to me.

"You know, you do some darn good work. I believe we can use you on our team."

He called management that day and they immediately added me to the HST LAN support group. Since I was already an employee, the paperwork was minimal, but in the process I discovered that I was switching to another side of Lockheed Martin. I was happy that I didn't have to go out job hunting and even happier to receive a five-thousand-dollar-a-year increase. My old managers were so happy that I had stayed to help wrap up instead of bailing on them that they gave me the entire contents of my office: my desk, chair, computer, monitor, and filing cabinet, enabling me to set up an office at home.

So now I was once again reporting onsite at Goddard Space Flight Center. It felt great to be back after almost a year away from the campus. I was even ok with sitting in a trailer behind Building 12. It was labeled Trailer 12A and we had to walk outside in order to enter the back of Building 12 and cross to the front to get to the restroom. That wasn't always good, particularly under adverse weather conditions.

I had a great team of sys admins now and we quickly grew close to each other and worked to pool our strengths so that we could quickly address any issues that would arise. I became very close to Shelton and Dave, and most of my training on server operations came from Shelton. We were working with a Windows NT server environment and had to learn installations of the server and workstation operating systems. Shelton was highly skilled in this area, but he didn't believe in holding anyone's hand too long, waiting for them to catch on.

After showing me the procedures a couple of times, he took me to Building 3, into the control center for Hubble, and showed me some systems that needed to be configured for the HST network.

"You should know this by now," he said, "so I'm going to leave you to it while I take care of something else." With that he turned and walked away, leaving me to navigate the waters alone. I was able to successfully install all of the systems necessary and configure all of them with the proper software and security settings.

My first solo job had been a complete success. From there I accelerated into every aspect of the support team.

Chapter Twenty-Five

Around this time we found out that my sister-in-law Sonia was battling cancer. She and Mike were soon engaged in a fight for her life. It was heartbreaking to witness the burden she had to bear. She was such a loving person and never had anything but kind words for anyone. Even if others were engaged in gossip or backbiting, she refused to participate. She had two little boys into whom she poured all of the love she could muster. She was faithful to God and to Mike, whom she truly adored. She faithfully attended Queens Chapel, and since Mike was not always around, she was often referred to as the lady with the two little boys. Allen and Adam were around eight and one, respectively, when her battle began, and she never let on to them what she was going through.

I began to pray with her a great deal and asked her to trust and believe that she would be healed. I gave her scripture to look up and taught her my favorites to use in the time of storm, Isaiah 53:5 and I Peter 2:24. I used to go and spend every Sunday after church with her and Vernetta. I would stay all day, until late and we had to think about work the next day. When Shari was off work for the weekend, she would come with me, and when she worked, it was just me, Brittany, and Brooke. Brooke was only a year old then, and Sonia was so weak at that stage that she didn't do much beyond hanging out on the couch, watching her boys and a little television.

One time, I went upstairs for something and when I came back down she was lying there, with Brooke sitting on top of her. They were just staring at each other and smiling. How I wished I had a camera. Brooke was quite a chubby little baby, so I asked Sonia if she was too heavy for her.

"No, we're just fine."

So I just watched them until I could tell she wasn't comfortable anymore and then I took Brooke down and off she waddled to find the boys.

One day, I showed her our wedding video, pointing out how she was tipping around, making sure everything was getting off properly, and again I saw her smile. She had been fighting for about two years now, yet the prognosis was getting dimmer. She called me on the phone one night, around two in the morning, crying profusely. Mike wasn't home and she was worried for him, her babies, and just the entire situation. I talked to her as long as she wished to stay on the phone, and after she'd had her cry, she calmed down and assured me that she would be ok. I couldn't help but cry a little myself after she hung up the phone.

We used to take turns carrying Sonia to the doctor to give Mike a chance to handle his business and to take some stress off. He had been working with his trucks and working on cars for other people to keep money coming in. One day I took her to the doctor, and when she came out, she was very sad. As I wheeled her chair out to the car and loaded her up, she said to me, "Well, the doctor said everything has spread, so I guess I'm not healed."

I could hear the defeat in her voice and no longer knew what to say. When we got back to her house and I brought her in, Mike was there. She reached out to him for a hug and told him what the doctor had said. After that, she deteriorated very fast, and in a couple of weeks they took her back to the hospital for the last time. By the next morning she was gone and our hearts were broken. She was taken back home on the Shore for burial, and the memorial service was very nice.

When they brought her out of the church for interment, I saw the tent and the hole they had prepared for her toward the rear of the church grounds and I lost it. I went off in the opposite direction, trying hard to keep it quiet within me, but I was spotted by Candy, who asked if I was ok. We hugged, and I cried like a baby. When I saw Shari, I immediately went and fell into her arms for comfort.

Sonia was only thirty-six years old when she passed, and Mike was devastated to the point of having to leave Allen and Adam with Mom for a while. The boys weren't faring very well either, not having their mom around. Sometimes Allen would just walk around the perimeter of the yard by himself, leaving us to wonder what he was going through. Adam would wake up crying at night and Mom would have to console and hold him to coax him back to sleep. They were fortunate to have their grandmother to rely on. It may have been nearly a year before Mike took full custody of them again. Seeing the boys all grown up now, I can't imagine the true cost of having lost their mom so early on in their lives.

Chapter Twenty-Six

Shelton and Teresa became great friends with Shari and I, so we began to spend a lot of time hanging out. We took trips together and celebrated birthdays by going out to various restaurants. We picked the most exotic or odd places to go when celebrating Shari's and Shelton's birthdays, which fell on the same date. Shelton and Teresa are a crazy, fun-loving couple and we spent almost as much time hanging with them as we spent with Larry and Debra, enjoying getaway vacations, cruises, and just hanging out for dinner. We've witnessed the birth of all of our kids and watched them grow through the years. It seemed that every time we traveled on vacations with Larry and Debra, one of the girls would be expecting, although sometimes we didn't find out until we got back.

We took so many trips to the Poconos that Shari and I became members of the Forever Lovers Club. They would give us free room upgrades, a bottle of Champagne, his and her towels, and sometimes a fire log. We loved to get the suites with the heart- or Champagne-glass-shaped bathtubs. We played miniature golf, table tennis, and pool. I was also able to talk Shari into paddle boating on a couple of occasions, despite the fact that she was terrified of little boats. they made her feel too unsafe, because she couldn't swim.

We also traveled to the Bahamas with Larry and Debra on a week-long all-inclusive vacation deal. We had a ball hanging out at the pool. It had a section with a bar that you could just swim right up to. We also took excursions around the island by bicycle to check out the beautiful buildings and the local casino. We ate ourselves silly, as all of the meals and drinks were included in the package.

One day we spent a couple of hours hanging out on the beach and got spooked by what appeared to be a snake or eel in the shallows, treading the water, watching us. Larry and I tossed rocks at it to encourage it to move on but it stayed right where it was. Eventually, Larry and I decided to risk a closer look, only to find, to our embarrassment, that it was a curved stick bobbing up and down in the water. We laughed about that for years.

Meanwhile, my work with the church was also growing. I was voted treasurer for the Male Chorus and provided computer support to Mrs. Hollis in the church office.

In 1993 the Male Chorus was invited to perform at the Congress of United Methodist Men, being held at Purdue University. It was my first time traveling with the group on a significantly long trip. We were there Friday to Sunday and our slot to sing was on Saturday. There were seminars held throughout the event and we managed to get in a little sightseeing as well. On Saturday evening we gathered for the keynote speech, and our chorus was scheduled to open it up with a couple of selections. The speech was being held in the performing arts center for all of the attendees and participants. The performing arts center was huge, and, we were told, a replica of Radio City Music Hall in New York City. I had never seen anything like it before in my life.

We stood backstage awaiting our time to come out and the anticipation grew with each second. Once we got the signal, we set ourselves up on the risers behind a closed curtain. When the curtain opened, I couldn't believe my eyes. There was a sea of people, about five thousand, from around the world, applauding expectantly. We sang two songs and at the end we were met with a roar from the crowd that lasted for what felt like at least ten minutes. When the curtain began to close, there were shouts of "Encore!" so the curtain halted.

The keynote speaker strode over to the podium amid the shouts, but the crowd would not settle down. He turned and gestured to us to perform another number and headed back to his seat as the crowd thundered even louder. We sang another song and were met with another ovation. I had seen standing ovations and cries for an encore before, but never from a crowd of this magnitude. We talked about the experience for many years after that.

Chapter Twenty-Seven

During this period, I was still heavily into softball and the Goddard league. I played with a couple of teams out there and had built quite a reputation for my speed and hitting ability. My control center formed a team that we named the Nimbuciles and we did pretty well in our early years. I don't recall ever winning first place, but we had a ball with Bob, Ricky, Iggy, Henry and the rest of the guys from the Nimbus project.

Our co-ed team pretty much dominated our league night for ten years. We had a blast with all of our friends on the team. With Thomas, Daniel, Shane, Timothy, Max T, Max B, Rodney, myself, and sometimes Darryl, there were no sharper guys on any team. Our girls consisted of Vanessa, Vicky, Lucy, Patsy, Betty, Benita, Rebecca and Gretta, who played equally as well as the guys. Wesley was our coach for quite a while and we combined for an unbeatable force for many years, and would have a blast clowning around and drinking beer at the shack after the games. Our men's league was fiercely competitive and I had a blast playing there as well. I could hit a grounder in the infield and usually beat the throw to first base, and I could hit over the infield for easy base hits, but where I got most of my thrills was from watching the players take up positions closer to the infield because of my size or because I'd gotten so many base hits by dropping the ball in front of them. That's when I'd let it rip and swing for the fence. I bounced the ball off the fence a number of times, but I only cleared it once, and that was called a foul ball. I still probably have the record for in-the-park home runs.

Some of the guys called me the fastest man at Goddard, and this rankled some of the younger guys. They would try to compete with me during games, so if I hit through the infield and stretched it to a double, they would try to do the same. I could read which ones would try it, so if they hit to my side of the field, I would get a good jump on the ball, and many times I threw them out at second base.

There was one kid who played on his father's team who resented the success I was having and the attention I was getting. I stretched one of my hits into a double, hitting through the right side of the field, so he decided he would try the same thing. When he hit the ball, I got a good jump on it. His father, realizing he was intent on scoring a double, screamed, "Take the one! Don't do it!" The young man, however, clearly had his mind made up, and everyone watched as he rounded first and headed for second.

I threw a beautiful line drive to second base, beating him out by two or three steps. The league's no-slide rule meant he was forced to stand up and take the tag like a man. His father was still screaming at him, "I told you not to do it! That guy has a very strong arm and you are not going to beat him out!" The young man was so upset that he took a bat and beat up the trash can.

The next time we were on the same field he challenged me to an all-out foot race. The guys on both teams were telling him

Chapter Twenty-Seven

to forget it, but that only made him more insistent, so they suggested that we position ourselves in the outfield and race to the first base line.

When we heard "Ready, set, go," we tore off for the infield. By the time we reached the finish line, I was a good ten feet ahead. That was the last time he asked for a one-on-one competition, but having accepted his loss gracefully, he and his father often called to invite me to play with them on weekends and in tournaments. I had a ball playing all over the county, and periodically I'd receive calls to come out and play with the Millers' team. They were known all over Maryland and typically won the local tournaments.

Then, at one of our Goddard Men's League games, I was having a great day on offense, with a double, a single, and an in-the-park home run, and was up at bat again. I hit a line drive that the shortstop managed to block, but he struggled to get a good handle on the ball. It was now a race to beat the throw to first base.

I was flying toward the bag, but as I reached the base, the first baseman stepped across the bag to block me, even though he didn't possess the ball. I tripped over his foot and went tumbling head first into the dirt. My shoulder took the brunt of the impact and I was in so much pain I thought that I had broken my collarbone. I looked him in the face and saw no remorse whatsoever. It made me so mad that I fantasized about taking my bat to a few of his bones, but my arm was totally disabled. The day was over for me. I had to have a pinch runner take over for me. I ended up in the emergency room. While my collarbone fortunately wasn't broken, my arm was in a sling for about two weeks.

I continued to have problems with my joints, with my right shoulder and right hip deteriorating to the point of needing surgery and eventually I was forced to get a total hip replacement. That marked the end of my team sport engagements, so I settled for coaching our co-ed team. Man, was it rough not to be able to get out there and shake it up with the crew.

The damage to my joints from the spill I took playing ball was serious enough to necessitate my seeing an orthopedic specialist. My shoulder required urgent attention. Avascular necrosis was the diagnosis, which is the death of bone tissue due to a lack of blood supply and oxygen, likely brought on or accelerated by sickle cell anemia because, during crisis, the blood flow gets clogged at the joints where the blood vessels are the narrowest.

So, even though I was no longer experiencing crises, my years of affliction had begun to catch up to me, although having someone deliberately trip you while you're running the bases was sufficient to cause such damage.

My doctor decided to try a procedure called a core decompression, where a surgeon would drill holes strategically through my shoulder joint, and then, as it healed, it would allow new vessels to form. Once again, my arm was in a sling, this time for about five weeks. After the first couple of days I felt strong enough to drive again so I went to the Male Chorus rehearsal and afterwards dropped by the Lomax's house for some soup and then headed home just before eleven o'clock.

I wasn't in a hurry, and with my right arm in a sling, I wasn't about to start playing around with the Hurst/Olds either. About a mile before my Woodlawn exit, on I-695, my car suddenly lit up with red and blue lights. I instinctively glanced at my speedometer to confirm I wasn't speeding, and pulled over, wondering what the problem was.

Chapter Twenty-Seven

It was the state police and the guy was huge. He asked for my license and registration and got somewhat irritated because it was a struggle to pull them out with only my left arm. He said he had been following me for a couple of miles and that I had been speeding. I politely disagreed.

"No, I wasn't speeding because I was in the slow lane the entire time. I'm not in any condition to be speeding, but another car did blow by me pretty quick. Are you sure you have the right guy?" Now he was definitely irritated. I thought that maybe some small talk might loosen him up, so I asked him if he knew either of my brothers.

"No, I don't know them," he snapped, and then hesitated. "What are their names?"

"Darryl and Kenneth Collins," I replied, and told him where they worked.

"No, I don't know them."

I let it drop, mainly because I was irritated that he had targeted me. My car has, on occasion, caused an officer to pull me over, but it was usually more out of curiosity and wanting to get a closer look. This guy struck me as more likely attempting to fill his quota.

Without further chit-chat, I signed the ticket, having already decided that I would take the citation to court.

After about a month, I got a notice with my court date. When the day came, I was more nervous than I had anticipated. I'd had my share of tickets in the past, and normally if I showed up in court, I would plead guilty just to avoid the points on my license. This day I was determined that I was not going to make that plea.

I sat in the courtroom, nervously waiting and looking around. It dawned on me that I didn't see the officer who wrote me the ticket anywhere. As the minutes ticked by, I began to hope that my case would be called quickly, so I could plead not guilty before the officer arrived, as the judge would automatically dismiss the charge. As luck would have it, as the time neared for my case to be called, I spotted the officer walk through the door.

When my name was called, the judge asked for my plea.

"Not guilty, Your Honor," I said with a confidence I didn't feel. I was sworn in and listened to the officer recount the events of that night. I frowned when he claimed that I had been driving in the secondary lanes, which meant a left or passing lane. I knew I had only driven in the slow lane. He claimed to have tracked me for about three miles, during which he said I had been driving consistently ten miles over the speed limit.

The judge asked me if I had any questions for the officer and I said yes. I asked the officer precisely what he meant when he said "secondary lanes."

"The left lane."

"Were you using radar to track my speed?"

"No," he admitted. "I was going by my speedometer."

"And when did you last have your speedometer calibrated?"

He hesitated and admitted he didn't know.

"And can you confirm the time you testified you pulled me over?"

He checked his notes and repeated what he'd said.

"Your Honor, I never once drove in the secondary lanes that night," I said, explaining that I had intentionally remained in the far right lane because my arm was in a sling. I also pointed out that the time he claimed he'd stopped me was incorrect, a fact, I further noted, was confirmed by the time that was written on the ticket itself, in his own handwriting. I wanted to cast doubt on the accuracy of his entire version of the events.

The judge was looking at the computer in front of him.

"You seem to be quite at home with these proceedings. Tell me about your record."

"Yes, Your Honor. I have received other tickets in the past, but I have owned up to any offenses I had actually committed. And I've gone to driver's school. But as a result, I haven't had any other tickets in over ten years. I'm married, with kids now."

"Hmm. I guess you found Jesus too."

"Yes, actually I did," I said, before I could stop myself.

The courtroom burst into laughter and I knew I was in trouble. The judge gave me a hard look.

"I'm feeling lenient," he said, "so I'm going to raise the fine to three hundred dollars."

I swallowed hard. That was more than double the original fine.

"I'm going to suspend the fine," he added, "and if you get another ticket within the next three years—for any infraction whatsoever—you will be required to come back and pay this fine. The points are also suspended."

With that he slammed the gavel and I was dismissed. I signed some papers and left the courthouse feeling a mixture of relief and upset. I was convinced that the officer knew he had falsely accused me, and the judge was trying to save face for the officer by grandstanding.

Well, I said to myself, I've gone ten years without a problem, so it shouldn't be too difficult to get through another three. I thank God that those three years came and went without further incident.

Chapter Twenty-Eight

The core decompression procedure on my shoulder was quite successful, and I was soon able to realize almost a full range of motion of my arm without pain. All the while, however, my hip continued to degrade. One day I went to Building 29 to assist a customer and as I attempted to climb the stairs, I experienced horrible pain in my hip and was forced to sit on the stairs and scoot up backwards, one step at a time. That's when I knew that I had to do something about the hip. This spelled the end of karate for me, which was a great disappointment.

After seeing my surgeon and setting a date for the procedure, I let management know that I would be out for at least six weeks. Because of the amount of work I routinely handled, they would need to bring someone in to cover.

Once that was done, and I spent a few days training my temporary replacement, I headed off for my surgery. I was much more nervous this time, because it was a much more intricate procedure compared to my shoulder work. The doctor asked for permission to give me blood in the event that I lost too much while under the knife. Reluctantly, I said ok.

Chapter Twenty-Eight

The next morning I was there bright and early for the scheduled surgical prep, with Shari by my side. My nerves got more and more frazzled as the morning progressed. Throughout my life, I have developed a hatred for needles, whether it was a shot for pain or a blood withdrawal. Drawing blood was the worst for me because all my veins seemed to shrivel up anytime someone approached with a needle. I watched with trepidation as they tried to insert an IV. When the third attempt failed, I got upset, having warned them at the start that they needed their most experienced phlebotomist to insert the needle, watching my arms turn black and blue. I told them I didn't want anyone else cutting their teeth at my expense, so they agreed to have my doctor or the anesthesiologist take care of it in the operating room.

They roll me in on a gurney and transfer me to the operating table. The room was bustling with activity and the sheer brightness of the lights hurt my eyes. It was uncomfortably cold as well, but they covered me with warm blankets, which was heavenly. I was smiling on the inside.

The anesthesiologist arrived and effortlessly inserted the IV into my arm. When the surgeon walked in, everything began to move very swiftly. The intravenous anesthesia felt like fire shooting through my veins. Startled, I yelped at the pain, but within seconds, I was out like a light.

When I opened my eyes, I was in an unfamiliar hospital room and it looked rather late, almost nighttime. My legs were strapped to a V-shaped pillow and the only position I could tolerate was lying flat on my back. As always, Shari was there to greet me when I opened my eyes. She stayed until visiting hours were over before heading out to get the girls from Mom Doris. I was still rather groggy after the sedative and had no trouble sleeping through the night.

When I awoke the next morning, they gave me breakfast and right away they began to get me moving. The first thing they did was roll me over on my left side and that's when reality set in that I had been through major surgery. My legs were still strapped to the V-shaped pillow and lying on my side forced my right leg in the air. It felt like someone was literally ripping me apart. I cried out but they continued whatever it was they were doing before eventually lowering me back to my original position.

Before lunch they sent me down the hall for a rehabilitation session. There I was instructed through basic exercises to get my leg muscles moving. It was painful and difficult to get through the routine, so I wasn't particularly enthused when they sent me down again for a second session later that afternoon.

The doctor came in and told me that the surgery had been a great success, that I'd hardly lost any blood at all, so the transfusion had not been necessary, and that he expected me to get twenty years out of this implant. That, at least, was good news after what my day had been like so far.

After the second day they decided to release me and set up visits to my home with the therapist. I was instructed to use a walker for the first couple of weeks and I got Shari to take me out to see the Male Chorus perform at the PG County Fairgrounds. It was a beautiful, warm, and sunny day and it did me a world of good just to get out of the house. The guys sounded awesome as usual, and they came over after their session was over. I got the usual jabs of jokes, like warning me about making my wife mad the next time, and so on.

Chapter Twenty-Eight

The rehab for my hip was a much slower process than that for my shoulder. I could not lie on my side or raise my right leg straight up hardly at all. My doctor initiated electroshock therapy to stimulate the muscle. I didn't like it, but it proved to be effective, as my sessions began to improve rather quickly after that. After about five weeks I only used a cane from time to time.

When I returned to work after six weeks, I kept the cane with me as a precaution. And now that my sickle cell disease had subsided, I could now travel, when before I was warned never to fly. Among the places we visited were South Africa, Zimbabwe, London, and Hawaii a second time, thankfully no crisis the second time. I even landed in Germany once, although we never got off the plane. All were wonderful—beautiful, spiritual experiences.

One of the most memorable was our trip to South Africa and Zimbabwe. Bishop May had invited the Male Chorus to travel with him on an exciting missionary journey to Africa. In South Africa we visited the beautiful city of Cape Town with its brilliantly white buildings against a backdrop of breathtaking mountains. In sharp contrast were the shanty towns, with homes held together with sod and wood, their tin roofs anchored with old car tires. The level of poverty was heartbreaking and often we found ourselves giving our jackets or hats to the natives just because they asked. Most of the homes we entered had dirt floors and a makeshift stove for cooking comparable to an open campfire.

We went to the Cape of Good Hope and it was spectacular! The views from the great cliffs overlooking the water were tremendous and we were told it was the point where the Indian and Atlantic Oceans met. We also visited a nature reserve there and the wildlife was almost equally spectacular.

When we got to Zimbabwe, we visited the African University and learned of the impact that the United Methodist Church has had on the continued operation of this historic and vital school of higher education. While standing outside preparing to leave, Phillip Gibson whom we all called Uncle Phil, began belting out "I Can Tell the World." This eighty-seven-year-old gentleman, who had become somewhat of a celebrity on our trip because most Africans in that area had never seen any man attain such seniority, proudly proclaimed, "I can tell the world about this. I can tell the nations I'm blessed. Jesus has made me whole and He brought joy, joy, joy to my soul." We joined in with a beautiful a cappella rendition that stayed with us until he passed away at age ninety-nine.

We visited a United Methodist Women's Retreat, where we were scheduled to sing. The location was not really a venue of sorts, but, rather, a large flat area outdoors with a lavatory consisting of nothing more than holes in the ground in which to relieve oneself. They had laid out chairs under a huge white tent and, although we didn't see any homes in sight, women dressed in white emerged from every direction, some with baskets on top of their heads that they never once reached up to steady or hold in place.

As the service began, we sat there on a platform at the front of the tent looking out over this massive site. There must have been nearly two thousand women present there that day, and when they worshipped, there was nothing like it on this planet. Their shouts and singing were like a war cry and you could feel the Holy Spirit riding on their hearts. Then something wonderful happened.

We were about to be called on to sing, and as we sat listening to the speaker, a whirlwind formed of pure white dust at the far end of the tent. It was not violent or noisy and we never felt the

Chapter Twenty-Eight

air move. We watched, spellbound, as it gently made its way down the center of the tent to where we were seated. It paused in front of the podium and then slowly dissipated before our eyes.

"God is in the building," I murmured, and those sitting near me nodded.

We sang our hearts out and the women danced and shouted to the Lord. It was a moment that I have never forgotten.

But that would not be the only miracle to occur on our trip. I got sick. I stopped at the front desk of the hotel one evening and purchased a bottle of water to drink and use to brush my teeth in the morning. I drank about half that evening before bedtime and saved the rest. When I got up the next morning, I brushed my teeth and opened the bottle to rinse, but before I took a mouthful, I was hit by a stagnant, almost rotten smell. I spat out the toothpaste and poured the bottled water down the drain.

By the end of the day I started feeling bad. By the next morning I couldn't get out of bed. I was having chest pains and fever, and I was convinced it was somehow connected to the water I'd drunk, and nothing to do with sickle cell. Pam kept tabs on me for the next couple of days, bringing me food and drinks and monitoring my situation. She asked if I wanted to go to a hospital or seek medical attention, but I declined. We were at the end of our trip and I had missed the last two days of activities and singing.

The next thirty-six hours was spent on flights back to the States, during which I was still quite weak and in pain. I slept through most of it and was never so happy to see BWI airport in my life. Shari and the girls were there waiting for me to come through the terminal and came running to greet me. I had to lean on Shari to get through baggage pickup and make it to the car. The next morning, I went to my doctor's office bright and early. I told him what happened with the water and he gave me a thorough examination. He said that my upper GI tract was swollen and the resulting pressure was the reason for the pain in my chest, and agreed that the likely culprit was the contaminated water.

He gave me an antibiotic and I was amazed at how quickly the pain and discomfort subsided. By the next day I felt like my old self, and there were no signs that I had any lingering problems associated with the effects of the water. All in all, I have no regrets. Traveling to Africa proved to be the experience of a lifetime and I am so happy to have had the opportunity.

Chapter Twenty-Nine

Shortly after returning home we got the good news that our family was growing once again. We had conceived about a month before I left on the trip but we didn't know until I returned and saw that familiar glow in my wife's face.

On April 12, 1999 Brandi entered the world as our last precious gift of life from God. She was beautiful, healthy, and full of smiles.

Once again Mom Doris and Pop Jerome were just beside themselves with delight in welcoming our new little bundle of joy. They would pick her up from daycare and watch over her until Shari or I came to take her home, just as they have willingly done since the birth of Brittany.

In 2001, word began to circulate that I hadn't had a crisis in ten years, and a young lady at our church approached me about it. A coordinator for the National Sickle Cell Association annual convention being held in Washington, D.C., that year, she asked if I would present my story at the event. I agreed.

I had to write a bio beforehand and I drafted notes for my speech. The convention was huge, and packed with people from all over the world. I spoke to a relatively large group primarily comprising doctors, nurses, and patients. The patients were enthusiastic, but the doctors sat silently, their skepticism that God had done what all the physicians in the world could not evident. I talked to people, both before and after my speech, and listened to presenters, but nobody I encountered knew of anyone else who hadn't weathered a crisis for even close to ten years.

I spoke again at the convention about five years later and the reception was still mixed. I couldn't tell them anything other than that God had blessed me with a miracle and felt it was a shame that more professionals couldn't, or wouldn't, acknowledge that God was responsible for my recovery and that there are no limits to His love or power.

At the end of June 2001, we joined friends on a cruise to Nova Scotia. Daria and her family had invited us to travel with them, and we invited Shelton and Teresa and their family to join us. We had a ball hanging out on the ship eating, catching shows, swimming, and watching out for all of our kids onboard, and then walking the streets of Nova Scotia, checking out all of the little shops and restaurants.

We sailed back to New York on Saturday and drove home to Baltimore, stopping first to check on Mom Doris and Pop Jerome. Mom Doris was sitting on the porch in her rocking chair, a big smile on her face as she watched our car pull up. Shari's brothers and her uncle Junie were there as well.

I walked back outside and joined Mom Doris. She appeared content and happy, rocking and humming. The next morning, back home, we headed out to church, followed by a stop at my sister Vernetta's. She loves to cook, and we often join her abundant "Soul Food Sunday" family dinner.

Chapter Twenty-Nine

There was no school on Monday, July 2nd, so Brittany and Brooke elected to stay at Vernetta's to hang out with their little cousin Tanya. Shari called Mom Doris to see if she might want to keep Brandi on Monday. I would drop her off in the morning on my way to work, and Shari would pick her up after work that afternoon.

I dropped Brandi off around eight in the morning, and Shari checked in with her mom later that day to make sure that all was well. That afternoon, after feeding Brandi, Mom Doris put her down for a nap and she sat down next to her with a book of crossword puzzles, dozing off herself at some point.

When Shari came in, she saw her mother and Brandi both asleep and whispered, "Mom, I'm here." Her dad, her brother Ronnie, and her uncle Junie were home. Around 4:30 p.m., Shari was surprised that her mother was still asleep despite there being enough noise in the house to typically rouse her. She watched her intently for several moments and then called to her to say she and Brandi were getting ready to go. There was no response.

Shari placed her hand on her to gently wake her up. When she didn't respond, Shari became alarmed and gave her a shake, calling out, "Mom! Mom!" The rest of the family came running and called 911.

Shari called me at work, hysterical.

"Shari, slow down. I can't understand what you're saying."

Someone took the phone and told me the paramedics were taking Mom Doris to St. Agnes Hospital. In the background, I heard someone say, "They say she's gone," and I could hear Shari crying. I yelled, "Tell Shari I'm on my way!"

I bolted out of my office, leaped into my car, turned on my emergency flashers, and weaved my way through the parkway traffic as fast as I could, managing to make it in less than thirty minutes, despite rush hour traffic.

When I reached the emergency room and raced to her bedside, I found everyone gathered around Mom, who lay there, eyes closed, an unattached tube in her mouth. At that moment I knew she was gone. I held Shari tightly as she sobbed. The last and youngest of Shari's siblings, Jerry, arrived moments later. He gasped when he saw his mother and all of us standing there, crying. He almost collapsed when he reached the bed. We were all inconsolable.

The next week was extremely hectic, trying to organize the service, and I tried to take as much of the burden off the family as I could. Shari's brothers, Ronnie, Steven, Larry, and Jerry, and her dad, were all happy to defer to Shari concerning the arrangements. Mom Doris had written a bio on herself for one of Brittany's school projects, which made putting together her obituary mercifully simple, and Shari and her family chose one of her mother's favorite suits for the funeral.

Family and friends continued to come from all over to help and support, bringing copious amounts of food in constantly, and the steady stream of visitors helped distract the family and keep their spirits up. The funeral at New Psalmist Baptist was beautiful and very large. Mom's burial was scheduled for the veterans cemetery, because of Pop Jerome's status, and she remained at the funeral home until Monday to complete the interment.

The burial was private and the sacred rituals of the military were very moving. We took a great deal of consolation in the idea that she had passed so peacefully, doing what she loved, sitting with her granddaughter as she slept, her beloved crossword puzzles in her lap. The doctors said the likely cause was heart disease, and nobody sought to have an autopsy performed.

Rest In peace, Mom Doris. We miss you and we love you.

Chapter Thirty

※

It was a miracle that I managed to travel the BW Parkway to Baltimore as fast as I did on the day that Mom Doris passed, as it wasn't unheard of for a delay to add an hour or two to your commute in rush hour. It became so tedious at times that I found myself getting really tired on the drive, and consequently I had a couple of mishaps where I wasn't able to stop in time when the traffic ahead of me suddenly ground to a halt. Fortunately, no one was hurt and the damage was minor. However, after two fender-benders and one instance where a young lady slid out of a side street into me on an icy roadway, my insurance company canceled my coverage. A new policy with my history proved extremely expensive, and after a couple of years and a couple more near misses, I decided I couldn't take the drive anymore. I was either risking killing myself or someone else, something that was just too awful to contemplate. I told Shari it was time to move.

The housing market was booming at the time, a real seller's market. I mentioned it to Mrs. Shirley one day and she began scouting for properties for us. We put in bids on some good prospects, but our contingency on selling our existing home meant we lost out to other bidders. Our real estate agent showed us homes

Chapter Thirty

around Largo and Lake Arbor, but prices had skyrocketed. She mentioned a new listing nearby, in a location known as both Bowie and Mitchelville, on one of our outings, one she hadn't had a chance to see yet, and we decided to take a quick peek at it.

It grabbed our attention at first sight. It had character. The owners were home, and welcomed us warmly. Our realtor, not having screened the property beforehand, had no real idea what to expect.

The main floor featured a foyer that was open all the way up to the roof. The stairs were adorned by paintings of famous figures in black history. The living room and dining room were off to the right, and as you walked straight ahead, you entered the kitchen/dinette area. On the the left was a nice family room with a wood-burning fireplace, and just behind the dinette area was a sliding glass door leading to a cozy sunroom. The basement was spacious, complete with an entertainment center and a pool table. I immediately thought, "Sold!" but I kept my mouth shut, imagining myself in my new man cave.

Upstairs were four bedrooms, the smallest almost comparable in size to our current master bedroom. The other two additional bedrooms were roomy enough for full-sized beds and furniture. The main bathroom was equally accessible to those three bedrooms, to the right of the stairs. It was not a huge or particularly luxurious bathroom, but it boasted double sinks, a tub, toilet, large mirror, and a linen closet. I was impressed. It was a huge leap from what we had in Baltimore.

When we walked into the master bedroom, we were blown away. It held a king-sized bed, complete with dressers and nightstands. There was also a built-in bookshelf and high nooks containing artificial plants, which added life to the room. The walk-in closet was insanely large compared to what we had at home, which was barely enough to store a broom and dustpan.

The master bathroom also had double sinks, and featured a huge mirror running the length of the wall, and the tub and shower opened around the corner, offering added privacy. The toilet was to the left of the doorway and had its own door.

My heart sank. This was certainly way out of our price range, and when I heard Shari say, "I really like this house," I felt even worse. Of all the houses we'd looked at, she had never made such a comment, not even on the ones we put in bids for. Some had been much newer, and some much bigger homes, but this was the only one that really called to us. Maybe it was because the house was so nicely staged, with furniture and décor that she could imagine herself living in. Most of the other homes were already vacant or not nicely furnished.

We chatted with the owners who said that they had raised their three kids there, and there had never been any problems in the neighborhood. They offered to install new carpet upstairs and, if we wanted to, we could choose the color.

I had to find a way to buy that house for Shari, I thought, but I still didn't know what the asking price was. We left the house, Shari smiling, and the realtor excited that Shari, who had never given much feedback before, clearly liked it, riffled through her papers and pulled out the listing to show us the asking price. To my amazement, it was less expensive than any of the houses we'd seen and we hadn't been impressed with any of those. Admittedly, the home was considerably older than comparable ones on the market. We put in a bid immediately, offering what they were

Chapter Thirty

asking, and in less than a week they accepted our offer, complete with its selling contingency. They told us that another family had bid a higher price, but requested that the owners put a door on every room, which made me wonder if they had been planning to house multiple families there. The owners liked us and thought we would be a perfect fit for the neighborhood. I'd say that it was God's favor once again.

We arranged an inspection, which flagged only minor items that needed attention, all of which the owners took care of immediately. Our next challenge was to sell our current home.

Our house in Baltimore was decidedly too small for us now anyway, making the move the right idea, but we had made a lot of improvements, so much so that I regretted having to relinquish it. We had remodeled the kitchen with new cabinets, floor, counters, dishwasher, range, and refrigerator—even the washer and dryer were new. And the icing on the cake was central air conditioning. We had installed a brand-new central air and heating system, and the house had never had air conditioning before.

Now we were about to leave it all behind, although our sadness was mitigated by our excitement over what we were headed into. We had spent seventeen years there and had clearly outgrown the two bedrooms and nursery area that we couldn't quite call a bedroom. Both properties had the same sized lot though, half an acre. The scary part was that we were trading an eight-hundred-dollar-a-month mortgage for a nearly three-thousand-dollar one, in large part due to the current high interest rates. God had blessed us with continued employment and growing salaries, but this would indeed be a test.

The house was very slow in getting hits, so I did a couple of things to give it more appeal. I dug up the broken sidewalk since it ended just a few feet into our property. I put down soil and planted grass to make the front yard nice and neat. I cut out the dead hedges across the front of the house that a tree had fallen on a couple of years back and put up a brand-new mailbox. Then I rented a sander and buffer and resurfaced the hardwood floors throughout the house. After that, prospective buyers who came in to view the place commented on how great the floors looked, but I suspected the tiny bedrooms were still a deal breaker for most.

In September we stepped out on faith and went to settlement on the Bowie house without having sold the old one. We were now new owners on Romsey Drive and there was no turning back. The girls were going nuts about getting to the new house and had already picked out their rooms. Every day they asked, "When are we gonna move?"

I called my brothers, along with Shelton and Larry, and asked them to come help us move the following Saturday. All week long we packed and cleaned, and I loaded up the car and made several trips to the new house with small things. I negotiated with the sellers to sell us their living room and sunroom furniture, and all of the paintings along the stairs.

When the guys arrived that Saturday, we loaded Michael's big boxed-in trailer with everything we could and whatever didn't fit we loaded onto our pickup trucks and headed down the beltway. We had so many helpers that everything was unloaded and moved inside in record time. It was a joy to settle into our new location.

Thank God for His grace and mercy once again, because as soon as we moved, we got an offer on the old house. They asked for two concessions. One was that the swimming pool in the backyard be removed, and the other was that we replace the shed out back. The pool was a large above-ground unit nearly five feet deep with a large attached deck surrounding it. I had thought it would have been a selling point.

I called my brother Moon and asked him to help me take the pool apart and haul it away. To my amazement he and Kenny showed up, took the pool apart, ripped out the old shed and the wired dog pen, and hauled it all away. Moon reassembled the unwanted pool in his backyard and I had to admit it looked better than ever. Way to go, Bro!

I purchased a new metal shed from Home Depot, and with the help of Shari's brother Stevie, assembled it. It took a couple of days to complete, and we had already closed on the sale before we finished. Having seen the way we handled the pool and the cleanup, the buyers felt confident that the shed would be finished to their expectations. It was my personal goal to please them.

When I returned, the house was already officially theirs and I felt proud that it looked in mint condition, ready for their move-in. I did one final walk-through while I waited for Stevie to arrive to help me finish the shed. I opened the basement door, hit the light switch, and gasped. I couldn't see the floor. There was water everywhere I looked.

"No!" I shouted. "No, no, no!"

We had never once had water in the basement for all of our seventeen years there. My nose told me it was sewer water. When Stevie arrived, we called the county sewage department. They came and checked the yard for a blockage but found none, but there was one up the street, over a block and a half away. Our house used to be the last on a dead-end street, but a year earlier, our street was extended and new homes had been built on a level higher than the preceding ones. Our old house now sat at the lowest point of the street and all of the new houses up the hill had been connected to the existing sewer lines, so when a blockage occurred, it naturally backed up at the lowest point and flooded our basement toilet. The water was almost a foot deep throughout the basement. They swiftly cleared the blockage first, naturally, and then got started on cleaning up the house. They came in with pumps and vacuums and got to work draining the water.

To my dismay, while they were working, the new owner arrived. It broke my heart to tell him what had happened to the house they'd just bought two days ago. I assured him that it had never happened to us the entire time we lived there, but I could well imagine what he was thinking, and knew that I would never believe any part of what I was telling him if I were in his shoes. He was appreciative of my concern and my efforts to take care of it, considering it was technically no longer my house, and I kept in touch to make sure the county treated him justly in the repair.

I'm glad I did, because at one point they tried to claim that the problem was on the property itself, and that they weren't responsible. I wrote a letter to the county and told them that Stevie and I were witness to the crew who, upon arrival and investigation, informed us that the point of blockage was up the street, and indeed we'd seen them working up there to clear it before returning to pump the water out of the house. They backed down. They had to tear out the paneling and the carpet and treat the walls against mold and mildew, but I'm happy to say that they did everything that was required to fully repair the house. I just pray that it never happens again. I was never a big fan of putting a new neighborhood right there among the old community. I had really enjoyed being "the last house on the left."

Chapter Thirty-One

Meanwhile, Shari and I had bought a timeshare unit at Orange Lake, in Florida. We decided to spend Thanksgiving there together with the Camper family, Larry and Debra, and our three godchildren, Lauren, Deidre and Larry Jr., who were no more than a year's difference in age between Brittany and Brooke. Brandi was the exception, being more than six years younger than Brooke. Both of our families ended up getting new SUVs as well, to make the trip, without either of us knowing what the other had in mind until we met the day before the trip to discuss logistics. We had bought a GMC Envoy and Larry and Debra had bought a Dodge Durango. We even gave them a portable TV to match the one we had so both vehicles could keep the kids entertained while traveling. The kids were head over heels in love with this new feature.

We hit the road on Saturday morning bound for Kissimmee, trailing each other in comfort and peace, making it to South of the Border in South Carolina, just beyond the border of North Carolina, and finally stopping for the night at the home of Debra's cousin, who was incredibly hospitable and loving, making sure we all had a comfortable place to sleep. The next morning, we set off

Chapter Thirty-One

early and, by evening, we had arrived at Orange Lake. We checked in, got our keys, and quickly found our unit and settled in. The unit was absolutely perfect, and the kids were so excited that we thought we would never get them to sleep.

It was a picture-perfect vacation. The resort had several swimming pools, complete with water slides, as well as a lake, tennis and basketball courts, a golf course, and various playgrounds. There was also an indoor gym and game rooms, along with a couple of little shops and a grocery store. Anything one might need could be found at the resort.

Still, we couldn't come all that distance, be so close to Orlando, and not take the kids to Disney World. It was an exciting day of rides, food, and shows. The biggest joy was watching Brandi go nuts over all of her favorite cartoon characters. We pushed her in a stroller to keep from getting separated and she didn't mind one bit. The Jaws movie ride was excellent, and downright scary. The twister exhibit was also off the hook. I don't know how they created a tornado right before our eyes. There were many attractions we were able to take in between Disney and Universal Studios. It was an awesome experience for the kids and adults alike.

We had done our food shopping for the Thanksgiving meal and much of the prepping had been done also. We elected to give each couple a parents' night out for one evening. Larry and Debra went first, while Shari and I watched the kids, and the next evening Shari and I attended a "Medieval Times" dinner and show. We had a great time and they gave us a souvenir picture as a keepsake.

Thanksgiving Day, I got up early to put the turkey in the oven, and then Debra and I started preparing the various side dishes, while the kids went off to the pool and the game room for a few hours, exploring and making new friends, until it was time to come back and get cleaned up before dinner.

As we gathered for prayer, Larry got emotional as he talked and prayed, thankful for our week-long adventure and saying that, for him, this special Thanksgiving meal was the icing on the cake. By the time he finished, it seemed like there wasn't a dry eye in the place. His kids teased him because they'd seen him get this emotional before. For us it was so touching to understand what it meant for us to be here, bonding as a single unit. It felt designed by God. We ate and toasted with sparkling cider and the evening went down as one of the greatest in all of our excursions together.

The next day was our last before hitting the road for home. The kids were off to their routine of swimming and frolicking around the grounds, and the adults kind of cruised around the facility, enjoying the warmth and taking in the sights while keeping an eye on the crew. The kids were on their best behavior and the week came to conclusion without any issues.

The next morning, Saturday, we loaded up and headed north. When we reached South of the Border on the Carolina border, we found a hotel to hole up in for the night and arrived, safe and sound, at home Sunday afternoon. As great as the experience was, it was a relief to be done with all of the driving. It would have been wonderful to have flown, but far more expensive. It was one of our lives' sweetest memories thus far.

Chapter Thirty-Two

By the time we moved to Bowie, both of our fathers had become very sick. My dad had heart surgery and a pacemaker implanted and Pop Jerome had been diagnosed with throat cancer. Both suffered for several years. Dad had renal failure and was forced to undergo dialysis for the rest of his life, while Pop Jerome's neck had become as hard as petrified wood and he could no longer turn his head. He also suffered kidney failure and was on dialysis. When Dad ended up in hospice care, we would run back and forth to the Shore to see him. After a while he became unresponsive and we knew then that it wouldn't be long.

On the last day I brought my anointing oil, and as we prayed, I anointed the room with oil, including the top of the doorframe, and asked God to keep out any negative, undesirable energy. Then I anointed Dad from the top of his head to the soles of his feet. He had not responded to anyone for a couple of days, but as I laid my hand on his forehead and prayed, he opened his eyes wide and stared at me. I gave him a big smile and praised God harder.

A nurse pushed the door halfway open as I was doing this, as if to enter, and inexplicably backed right out. It was as if God had an angel keeping the door and she probably had no idea why she couldn't cross the threshold. God's presence was so strong in that room and every word uttered by us was born of love and concern that entire afternoon.

As the time to depart and get back to the kids drew near, Vernetta chose to stay with Mom at the hospice center because Dad had started the transition and his pacemaker device kept kicking in to jumpstart his heart each time he started to crash. There was no way to know how long it would be before the device would no longer be able to restart his heart.

About one or two in the morning we got the call that Dad was gone. I held Shari in my arms and cried. Knowing what he had been through the last couple of years, and that when he tried to depart there was a device that kept shocking him back to life, I felt somewhat relieved for his sake that he had finally passed in peace.

On November 6, 2004, we held a beautiful service for Dad. He was carried to his final resting place by his sons and it seemed like everyone that I had ever known from childhood had come to pay their respects. It was the end of an era now that our patriarch had departed. There were enough loving memories of Dad to keep him alive in our hearts and minds for years.

Rest in peace, my beloved father.

The days that followed were difficult enough. I hadn't envisioned that it would get worse. Four days after the burial, we got a phone call early in the morning from Shari's brother Larry. Shari's dad, who had just gotten out of the hospital and celebrated his seventy-first birthday the day before, had passed away in his sleep at home. Shari was devastated.

I asked if she wanted to see him before they moved him. When we arrived at the house, friends and relatives had already begun showing up, as the news spread. We went upstairs to Pop's bedroom and found him curled up, under the covers, looking as if he were asleep.

The coroner had already been to pronounce Pop Jerome, and now the funeral home was coming to collect the body. As with Mom Doris, Pop's boys deferred all of the decision making to their adored "momma hen" sister. Their family has always supported one another, which meant there were no disagreements as to how things would be handled. I have no doubt that my own family loves one another deeply, but we tend to be highly competitive and could be a little aggressive toward each other. Still, I am grateful that when we need to pull together, we are as tight as it gets.

On the following Tuesday, November 16th, we held Pop Jerome's funeral service and he would be reunited with Mom Doris, the love of his life, at the veteran cemetery two days later. It was hard to fathom that in that three-year period, from 2001 to 2004, my wife had lost her mother, her uncle, her grandmother (Mom Mamie) and her father, along with my father—all in such a short span. It was a very difficult three years but through it all God sustained us and kept the family together.

Chapter Thirty-Three

My job continued to evolve over a period of thirty-six years at the Goddard facility, and I thrived amid my continuous service path with MATSCO, General Electric, RCA, Martin Marietta, and then Lockheed Martin. I had started out as a data clerk and moved through the positions of data technician, computer operator, UNIX systems administrator, network administrator, and then computing systems engineer. I was now giving computer and network support on the Hubble Space Telescope (HST) project and the James Webb Space Telescope (JWST) project.

My salary, it turned out, had been severely lowballed for the first twenty years of my career. And then one day I found myself reporting to a manager whom I believe was sent by God. Henry called me to his office and what he said left me flabbergasted.

"You're not even on our pay scale," he said, scratching his head. "We don't have a position here in the company that's paying as little as what you're making."

It turned out that I was training new hires and some not-so-new employees who were making more than double what I made, which was just under thirty-five thousand dollars a year. I thought back to when my then manager Joe gave me a promotion while insisting my pay be twenty-five cents an hour less than the minimum posted for the job. That's where it had started, and what a difference it made over the course of those decades.

Shari made more than I did, so although we didn't have much to set aside for savings, we had managed to buy our house from Vanessa, keep pretty decent automobiles to get us back and forth to work, and feed our three girls without a lot of stress and strain.

Henry initiated an instant six-thousand-dollar increase, with an additional twenty percent raise by the end of the year, , which was repeated annually for the next three years. I was saddened, but not surprised when Henry was removed without warning as our manager just a week after addressing this issue with me, and wondered whether it might have been done to make sure he was not reachable in the event that I decided to sue, something I had no intention of doing. Still, I was bothered that no one in my unit knew in advance or got to say goodbye. I had, in the course of my career, three managers who had impressed me with their integrity and impartiality: Dick Stephenson, Lee Sarsfield, and Henry Powers.

Meanwhile, I had held many positions within the church besides being treasurer for the Male Chorus. I had become a member of the United Methodist Men, the chairperson on Spiritual Formation, Worship Leader for the Sunday service, a member and later chairperson of the Church Council, Church Lay Leader, and president of the United Methodist Men. My experience in and around Queens Chapel was flourishing and I had a beautiful relationship with pretty much all of the congregation.

I've always tried to remain fair and impartial concerning every issue I was involved in that pertained to the church. I have a genuine fear of angering God after all that He's done for me, and I try never to pass judgment on anyone for fear of being judged myself.

I have enjoyed a close relationship with all of my pastors and I have seen a few come and go. After Rev. Kess retired, we received Rev. Dr. Bruce F. Haskins. He was the one who began to propel me through the various church offices. He was also the only one who put me in his pulpit to deliver the word in his absence. We had a very special and deep relationship. I never told him just how terrified I was of standing there in his absence though. Queens Chapel can be a very tough, honest and straightforward group of brothers and sisters. They have no problem letting you know if you screwed up or failed to follow protocol. I learned that being a pastor was a job that I hoped God would never call me into. I had great respect for that position and I always recalled 1 Chronicles 16:22: "Saying, Touch not mine anointed, and do my prophets no harm." For that reason I always gave the pastor the benefit of the doubt and tried to see and support his vision as anointed by God. If he was wrong or out of step with the Lord, then I had no doubt that God would deal with it. If there was something that I didn't agree with, I took it to them in private to ask them to clarify their position.

I came to learn before long that the close relationship that I thought I enjoyed with Rev. Haskins was the same relationship he had with essentially all of his congregation. He made us all feel special, and despite three heart attacks before he got to our church, he was the hardest-working pastor that I had ever seen, not to mention that his understanding and delivery of the word was brilliant.

After Rev. Dr. Haskins, we received Rev. B. Kevin Smalls, and, again, I enjoyed a very close relationship with our pastor. He had a very different vision of what God sent him to do compared to his predecessors, and his focus was on reaching the youth of the church. He understood that the future was in the children, and he tried to give them church that they could understand and enjoy. He didn't depart from all of the traditional pieces of worship that the aged of the congregation liked, but he changed us in a radical shakeup that helped us to also focus on the needs of our youth rather than look for self-gratification. He received his doctorate while with us and shortly afterward was pulled to shepherd a much larger flock in Indiana.

At present we have Rev. William Butler and it just has to be God at work in Queens Chapel because the congregation continues to grow and thrive. Rev. Butler has brought us back to an old-school type of fire and brimstone service, but his teaching, knowledge, and wisdom go far beyond what we have known. His grasp of the Word and his ability to teach and open our eyes to yet newer revelations in Christ Jesus is uncanny. All of our ministers have been exceptional in their own way, and have raised Queens Chapel to new and profound heights.

Chapter Thirty-Four

It was during Rev. Dr. Haskins' tenure at Queens Chapel that my brother David took a turn for the worse. He was living with Karen, his fiancée, when his illness began to escalate, just as mine had before God stepped in and took it away. I had no doubt that God would do the same thing for him. David's episodes became more and more severe, starting in November of 2005. That January, David found himself in Peninsula Regional Medical Center, right through February. Our mom had traveled to Hawaii with our sister Belinda so, while there, she called her pastor to ask if he would visit David and pray for him in her absence. The pastor ignored her request and, in fact, was very indignant with her throughout the call.

David's condition was not improving, so we had him flown out of Salisbury up to the University of Maryland Shock Trauma Unit. While he was there I asked Rev. Haskins if he would visit David to have prayer with him. To my surprise he not only visited David right away but returned over and over again. David began to recover and would tell us about the tall, great preacher who had stopped by to see him. He started asking questions about God and we gave him a Bible and read to him when we visited. He began

Chapter Thirty-Four

to get really excited about it and he was soaking it up and growing in Christ. He was taken to John 3:16 and he gave his life to Christ.

He loved it when Vernetta and Cornelius, who were now deacon and deaconess, came to give him the Sacrament of Communion. He wanted to take it over and over again. When he was deemed strong enough, the hospital released him, even though they were not able to identify the source or type of infection he was suffering from. Apparently, it started after the hospital in Salisbury had given him a colonoscopy, but they denied it, even though his dangerous downward spiral began right after the procedure.

When David went home, I would talk to him on the phone about the Word and ways for him to get closer to God. One day I told him that if he really wanted to feel God's presence, he should go into the smallest available room—a bathroom or closet—and contemplate intently on what God meant to him. One day, shortly after that, he called me.

"I did it, man! I did it!"

"Did what?" I asked.

"I went into my closet and I felt the Holy Spirit!"

I knew from his excitement that he had experienced a true encounter. The first time I had the encounter, I was so frightened that I jumped up and ran. The next time I sat still and enjoyed the wonderful, tingling sensation of raw and awesome power.

After David's encounter, he developed a peaceful, confident demeanor that was very evident. Even though he still was pretty weak, he kept a smile, and visited with the family when some of us came home.

After a couple of weeks he regressed back into crisis, and at one point slipped into a coma for about two days. When he began to stir, he spoke as if he were still in a dream of some sort, to someone other than us.

"What is this room?" he asked. "Why are those people staring at me? They think that I'm afraid. I'm not afraid. It seems kind of peaceful here."

When he was fully awake, he told us that he had seen Sonia and Dad, who smiled at him. We wondered whether he had gotten a little glimpse of heaven. From then on, everything in his world was ok.

We were once again scrambling to have him transported to Baltimore, because we just couldn't trust the hospital in Salisbury. David assured us that it was ok this time, but we pushed to get him out and ultimately he was transferred by private ambulance to the University of Maryland. Karen, his fiancée, and a family member paid the expense, and Shari and I later reimbursed them.

David's condition continued to degrade until he was no longer responsive, and the doctors still had no clue as to what the infection was that had caused his organs to deteriorate to where his kidneys and liver no longer functioned. I had experienced this firsthand and so I still held steadfastly onto my faith that God would step in and give him back to us.

It got to where he had to be put on life support, and for the first two weeks, we waited, still holding out to give him and God a chance. Eventually, we gathered the family together to debate whether to disconnect him.

On the night that we decided to disconnect him from the machines, Rev. Haskins stopped in to pray with us. When he went to David and began to pray, there was no doubt that this man of God was filled with the power of the Holy Spirit. He laid hands on

David, and as he prayed, things began to happen. The machines sped up as David took over for himself and opened his eyes. He tried to speak but the tubes in his mouth and throat prevented it, so he tried to pull the tubes out. By now, the nurses had come running, because they saw his monitors light up.

They grabbed his hands to prevent him from removing the tubes, and Karen and I pleaded for him to calm down and lie still. He forcibly shook his head no to us. They strapped his hands down so that he couldn't pull the life support out, and after a while, he stopped struggling. We all took turns talking to him, and each time he shook his head no. Once each of us had taken our turn trying to reason with him, he lay still, unresponsive. All the while Rev. Haskins stood, silently observing.

We discussed whether David might have been begging us to disconnect him, and the reasons why, and decided that it did seem as if that was what David wanted, that if we were to put it into David's and God's hands, His plan would be revealed to us. If David was going to remain with us, he would not need the machines, we reasoned.

We informed the doctors that we wanted to turn off the machines and the nurses immediately complied. Some of us watched as the systems were disconnected, while others went off to reflect. I desperately wanted to believe that David wanted the tubes removed because he didn't need them to remain with us. But, instead, David departed within minutes of being unplugged. It was one of the most painful moments in my life, watching him go. It looked as if he had tried to mouth "Thank you," and then the next moment he was gone.

Karen and I remained by his bedside for a long time, praying, wishing that it hadn't had to be. He was so bloated and swollen that we considered whether it might be better to have a closed casket. At that point anyone who knew David but hadn't seen him in his final days would not have recognized him and would most likely be upset.

We pulled back the covers and were horrified by the appearance and condition of his body. There were open sores and huge blisters, some filled with fluid, on his stomach, back, and legs, as if the medicine they had pumped into him had merely pooled under the skin instead of circulating through his system.

Now my heart really was in pain. Real pain. Inconsolable pain. It was as if the part of him beneath the covers had begun to decompose before his spirit could be released. No wonder he was so desperate to remove the tubes. He could not have stayed with us any longer. His body just would not support him anymore. I ran out of the room, weeping, and I told my family that we should have let him go sooner, because there was no way he could have stayed. The events of May 26, 2006, were now burned into our hearts and minds forever.

We thought it would be a good idea to lay David to rest near Dad, in the Oaksville community cemetery. Since David and Karen were engaged but not married, decisions about his burial would be made by his mother. Mom was also the one carrying his life insurance. Karen was still included in all of the planning, contributing in any way she could, and she even contributed to covering the funeral costs. What we were unprepared for was when those in charge of St. Marks United Methodist Church, who exerted authority over the cemetery, decided they couldn't make room for David because he wasn't a member of the church. This was our church growing up, the church across the road from where we'd lived our entire life, where David and I often played outside. This was the community we grew up in, which recognized everyone there as a relative. The one place that I had some of my fondest childhood memories suddenly felt like a cold and hostile wasteland.

Indeed, the pastor had already alienated Mom when she asked him to visit David in the hospital. We met with those in charge to discuss why they didn't have room for David and found out that people had been donating sums of money to the church to secure a spot for themselves. We already knew that there were people buried in the cemetery who had never even lived in Oaksville, or been members of the church, but they were relatives of church and community members.

The more the discussion continued, the more I became convinced that I no longer wanted David, or any other person whom I loved in the world, to be laid to rest there, and found myself wishing Dad had been buried elsewhere. I left the meeting and crossed the road singing Isaiah 54:17, "No weapon formed against me shall prosper."

We approached Springhill Memory Gardens, in Salisbury, and bought four adjacent plots there. Mom would be buried there, we agreed, instead of near where dad was laid. Moon, myself, or anyone else who needed a place to lay would be able to go there, hassle free.

There was no question of our using St. Marks for the funeral after mom's experience with the pastor, and all ties were now fully severed. The University of Maryland Eastern Shore agreed to allow us to use their Ella Fitzgerald Center for the Performing Arts as the venue for the funeral and their dining hall for the repast. Friends and relatives from all over, including those in Oaksville, chipped in and helped however they could.

"No weapon formed against me…"

When it was time to go and view David at the funeral home for the burial approval, we were all on edge because seeing David's condition at the hospital made us think we could not allow him to be viewed. We approached his coffin apprehensively, but we were surprised and relieved that he looked a lot like himself, to where we could even safely have, we agreed, the coffin open for viewing. Bennie Smith Funeral Home had done an inspiring job.

"No weapon formed against me…"

I asked Rev. Haskins if he would consider officiating over the funeral, since he had been the closest minister to David through his transitioning, and he said that he would be honored to do so. I made reservations for the reverend to stay the night before at the college so he could relax and not be so hurried. I also asked my friends, the gospel group from Queens Chapel, The Lomax Sisters, who had gotten to know Mom over the years, if they would sing at the funeral and they agreed.

To my astonishment, on the day of the funeral, Queen's Chapel United Methodist Church, my church home for the last thirty years since I'd relocated from the Shore, showed up in the very motor coach I had rented to transport the Lomax Sisters. I was totally blown away by how many of them came to support the Collins family.

The service was everything we had hoped and prayed for, and all the answers I needed about why David had to leave us, and why my God didn't give David the healing that He'd given me became clear. There was a full line of pastors on the stage to support Rev. Haskins, all of whom spoke wonderful words of encouragement during the Words of Comfort segment.

Cousin Reggie sang his heart out with "I Won't Complain," and The Lomax Sisters blew everyone away when they performed, a cappella, "The Storm Is Passing Over" and "Rock My Soul in the Bosom of Abraham," and received a well-deserved standing ovation.

The service just kept building, and Rev. Haskins added the icing to the cake: We were all in tears as he explained what he had observed during David's transition. He said that David had been living, trapped in a broken building, and he was trying to let us know through the words of the old song "There's a Leak in This Old Building and My Soul Has Got to Move." He said David had shaken his head no to let us know that he had gotten a glimpse of his new home in glory and that he was sorry, but he had already packed up and was ready to go. Yes, he had "a brand-new building not made by man's hands." The message was indescribably eloquent, and we cheered and shouted through it all.

When the message was over, and Pastor Haskins symbolically opened the doors of the church, he called for anyone who wanted prayer to come forward. My heart lifted even further, as I watched people pour down to the front of the church for prayer. It dawned on me that they weren't just people—these were my brothers, my cousins, my uncles, and friends of David. David, I saw now, had a different purpose for being here than I had, and a different way of departing. My passing when I was at my sickest might never have touched as many people as in the way David had touched his family and friends.

My calling is to tell the world that God is still on the throne and He is still in the blessing business. His miracles and His Works are as true now as they were when Jesus walked, talked, healed, and saved, here on earth.

Rev. Haskins ushered the ministers from the stage toward the people gathered in front for prayer and guidance in salvation. One preacher needed a bit of prodding, I noticed, having sat through the service with a frown that was out of place among all of the worshipful congregants. It was the pastor of St. Marks United Methodist Church in Princess Anne/Oaksville. Why he had come I had no idea, and perhaps he was put out that he was not the one officiating this moving, uplifting service. Reminding myself of God's Word, "Saying, touch not mine anointed, and do my prophets no harm" (Psalm 105:15) was sufficient to ensure that nothing he did that day took away from the blessing that God poured over the entire day.

At the end of that unforgettable day, God gave me His final answer: *David belonged to me. I only loaned him to you. I allowed him to stay until his salvation was complete. I did not put him here to duplicate, complete, or validate your assignment. You must fulfill your promise to Me.*

My promise was that I would tell everyone I met about the miracle of my healing and the mercy that He has shown me. To take away a full-blown disease that was inherited from birth at the very time that it had done so much damage, to where death was imminent, attests to the fact that there is nothing too hard for my God.

We gathered outside after the service, preparing to take David to his resting place. The procession was so long that we were in awe. Even the bus with my church family went to the burial site, and after the interment they all returned to **UMES** for the repast. The mood was not sad at all, as some might have expected. Instead, it was a celebration and everyone was loving, supportive, and extremely helpful.

Our cousins had opened their hearts to us, and there was a ton of food and drinks, and many of them stayed on hand to serve it. I got a big kick out of my church family, who were amazed that they couldn't tell my mom from a couple of her sisters. When it was time for them to load up and head home, The Lomax Sisters serenaded Mom with "God Be With You Till We Meet Again."

To this day I smile as I recall the experience of witnessing David's home-going and the events surrounding his passing. It has always stayed with me that God has yet allowed me to witness another miracle. David is forever a part of me, the only sibling who shared and could fully relate to my pain and suffering. My life has been full of miracles as I consider the path that my God set me on and blessed me through. I understand that He has shown me great favor. I often hear folks say, "Favor isn't fair," so I am determined not to take His favor lightly, or take for granted where I am today. I have been protected from danger, spared from calamity, and saved from an illness that generally takes its sufferers out before adulthood.

Looking back at my sixty years, I have done and seen things I never dreamed that I'd ever get to experience. I met the love of my life and married her. I fathered children and have been blessed that not one of my four girls inherited my disease. Even though they carry the sickle cell trait and will need to be considerate of whom they choose as a mate, they have control over whether or not they will bring a sick child into the world. They have the advantage of knowing what the name is of the infliction that will shadow and threaten their happiness.

So far, Tina and Brittany have married mates who don't possess the trait, and so they have strong and healthy children. Brooke and Brandi have not started any families at this time and I praise God for that.

Shari and I eventually decided that a boy was not be in the cards for us, so it was time to close the factory. We never used birth control but I always prayed, "Lord, please don't let us get pregnant." It seems that He heard me every time.

At the time of this writing our baby Brandi is seventeen years old and, our bodies have taken the natural turn to where pregnancy is no longer a concern. I now have seven grandchildren and two great-grandchildren. I have traveled many places here and abroad, when the doctors said that I couldn't fly because of pressurized planes and thin air not enriched with enough oxygen. I have enjoyed hobbies like karate and racing cars. I have played sports both when I was susceptible to having the crisis and after the threat had been taken away. I managed to maintain a career and hold a job in continuous service for over thirty-seven years, no doubt solely through God's grace, considering the number of forced absences and long stays in the hospital that caused others elsewhere with my condition to be laid off or forced into disability. I also achieved a salary that I could never have imagined, one that would eventually break the six-figure mark. I have been praised for my job performance over and over, as well as received awards for mission success. I have witnessed firsthand instruments at NASA that would eventually change the world and technology as we know it. I have climbed the launch tower at Cape Canaveral and worked around the most powerful space vehicle known to man. I have touched three of the space shuttles that were preparing to embark on missions to service the most powerful telescope ever made. I have given testimony to God's awesome power, grace, and mercy in many churches all over the local area, as I traveled with the Male Chorus. I have stood in the pulpit and delivered God's word to His people and worked in almost every ministry of the church.

Out of it all, the most precious accomplishment in my life was witnessing souls being saved as the result of my testimony, or a word that God had me deliver to his people. I walk this life secure in the belief that only what you do for Christ shall last, and, as Luke 12:48 states, "To whom much is given, much is required." God has done so much for me that my gratitude knows no bounds, and while the favor He has shown me is beyond my understanding, I do understand my calling. I often asked the question "Why me Lord? Why are You so mindful of this little insignificant speck?" I believe now that the answer is simple. It is my purpose in life to remind God's people that "We do not wrestle against flesh and blood, but against principalities, against powers, against the rulers of the darkness of this age, against spiritual *hosts* of wickedness in the heavenly *places*." Ephesians 6:12

Yet be encouraged. We serve a God who has already ordained that we shall triumph. He is the all powerful, all knowing, able to be everywhere at the same time creator of all that was, is and is to come.

Simply put, I am required to let the world know that (as the Williams Brothers so eloquently sing), "I'm still here," on this earth, because He is still here.

Indeed, my life has been a portrait of miracles.